"Clara's book is not only functional, with excellent practices, but beautifully written with wonderfully moving stories. It's like taking a series of unusual excursions into the inner worlds of consciousness so that you can see how forgiveness occurs and how it benefits those brave enough to risk the journey."

—Ron Hulnick, President, University of Santa Monica, and, co-author with Mary Hulnick, of *Remembering The Light Within: A Course in Soul-Centered Living*

"This powerful, easy-to-absorb book is a welcome addition to the topic of the healing power of forgiveness. The moving stories of those that have experienced the 'unforgivable', the guided exercises and Clara Naum's unique coaching approach left me feeling lighter, more loving and more powerful just in the first read. *The Real Meaning of the "F-Word"* is something I will eagerly share with clients and colleagues."

—Rory Cohen, Founder of www.take10now.com

"An absolute masterpiece. With this exquisite work, Clara Naum challenges us, teaches us, and holds us lovingly as we step tentatively into the idea of forgiving the unforgivable. Her stories and examples light the way and make this very personal Soul-search accessible to all. This is an important work, much needed in our world today."

—Laura Dewey, Coach, Author, Educator

"Clara, at some point in the editing process it became clear to me why I was the one chosen to work with you. Your words are making a positive and profound impact on my relationships and my work. What you've written is empowering and transformative. I feel so grateful to be working with you!"

—Suzanne Potts, Creative Consultant, Editor

THE

# REAL MEANING

OF THE

WORD

ALSO BY
CLARA LEON-NAUM

*Spiritual Passport, Finding the Answer,* published June 2013

*Pasaporte Espiritual,* published September 2016

*Soul Journey to Freedom,* to be released January 2017

THE

# REAL MEANING

OF THE

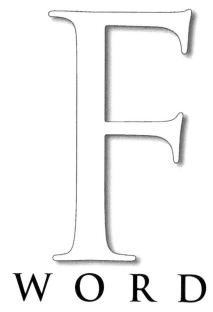

# WORD

FORGIVENESS AS A PATH
TO FREEDOM

CLARA LEON-NAUM

Printed in the United States of America

ISBN Paperback: 978-1536914795

Cover and Interior Design: Ghislain Viau

The Rumi poem "The Guest House" on page 115 is used with grateful permission of the translator, Coleman Barks.

# CONTENTS

# ACKNOWLEDGMENTS

To you my reader, who is eager for healing and will drink from each page, thank you for your time, your caring and your love!

To my husband and son, thank you for encouraging me to give birth to this book. I love you both so much! Thanks to you, I have learned the difference between love and unconditional love.

To my mother, who taught me to never give up and never lose faith, thank you for your love.

To my father, who smiles at me from someplace in heaven, thank you for teaching me the power of gentleness and kindness, no matter what.

I am grateful to all my clients. You have allowed me to do what I love, and you have inspired me to "walk my talk." A special huge thank you to all of you who allowed me to share your stories in this book. Your willingness to show that forgiveness and healing are possible even in the most difficult circumstances will help more people than we'll ever know.

I have learned from so many mentors and teachers, some I have known and some I have never met. Thank you for the wisdom and healing you have shared in your books and workshops! You have helped me be the person I am today.

Thank you to Drs. Bonnie and David Paul for coordinating the amazing Prison Project, Freedom to Choose. Participating with you in this service project has changed my life. I owe a most profound thank you to the courageous men and women I had the opportunity to serve in prison. You taught me the real meaning of forgiveness.

To Drs. Mary and Ron Hulnick, thank you for inspiring me to be myself. Completing my Master's in Spiritual Psychology at the University of Santa Monica was a joyful and enlightening experience that continues to shape my life every day, every step of the way.

To Dr. Robert Holden who through his numerous books and workshops continues to inspire me to choose happiness.

Thank you, Suzanne Potts and Melanie Votaw for your help editing this book. Our creative conversations and your attention to detail were a pivotal part of the process of making this book a reality.

It took me a year after I'd completed writing the book to make the decision to self-publish. I had to use my own medicine – The 3Fs Process – to release my self-judgment and forgive myself so that I could continue to move forward. Thank you, Rory Cohen and Laura Dewey from my Mastermind Group for encouraging me to finally give birth to this book.

Last but not least, I give thanks to God, my partner in life, who is always there for me, teaching and supporting me to live a forgiving life.

# INTRODUCTION

*"As high over the mountains the eagle spreads its wings,*
*may your perspective be larger than the view from the foothills.*
*When the way is flat and dull in times of gray endurance, may your*
*imagination continue to evoke horizons."*
—John O'Donohue

This book guides you through the 3Fs Process, a unique forgiveness practice I developed through my work as a Spiritual Counselor and Life Coach. This Process leads you on an inner journey *at your own pace* toward transformation and awakening. When we are no longer immersed in the stories we have told ourselves about what happened to us, when we leave the "victim seat," we have the opportunity to free ourselves from our pain and suffering. In freeing ourselves, we have the opportunity to choose empowerment, happiness and fulfillment instead.

Through my own story, as well as the stories of several of my clients, including a man who was raped as a child and kept it a secret until he became so ill he almost died, a prisoner who murdered his fiancée, and a Holocaust survivor, *The Real Meaning of the "F-Word"* demonstrates the power of forgiveness. The real *"F-Word"*, of course, is *Forgiveness*. Forgiveness is the easiest and fastest route to that other sweet *"F-Word:" Freedom*. Ultimately, going through the 3Fs Process gives us the opportunity to awaken to who we really are, and who we really want to be.

## How Does the 3Fs Process Work?

Before we can experience freedom and awakening, we have to say, "F**k it!" This also happens to be the first phase of the 3Fs Process. In the "F**k It!" phase, we acknowledge and work through our shock and anger at whatever we have perceived to be hurtful and/or unfair. We also acknowledge our natural desire to blame – others, ourselves and/or the circumstances. We dare to go into that dark place where we relive our pain in order to transform it. We learn to express anger in a healthy way.

If we tell ourselves to "just get over it" or "just forgive, forget, and move on," we suppress our hurt feelings, and often find ourselves attracting new circumstances that trigger the same hurt and bring up the same resentment. Only after we have acknowledged, worked through, released and transformed our anger and hurt can we move on to the second phase.

The second phase, or the "Full-Spectrum Forgiving" phase, is the core of the 3Fs Process. "Full-Spectrum Forgiving" is exactly what it sounds like. It is your chance to forgive across the board – to forgive everyone, including yourself! In this phase, we begin to see that the stories we tell ourselves, the stories we think make us who we are, are just stories, and that we can release or transform them.

The disempowering dramas that have held us in their thrall can be transformed into empowering tales of triumph. We have the opportunity to step out of the victim role and into our authentic power.

Once our stories have been acknowledged, honored, released and transformed through forgiveness, it's possible to take a higher perspective, to see our lives and ourselves from a different, more evolved vantage point. You may find yourself struggling mentally with the idea of letting go of old wounds that no longer serve you, but your heart will tell you the truth. Your heart wants to let go, to awaken to unconditional loving, which is truly only possible if ALL has been forgiven.

The third phase, or the "Freedom" phase, helps you anchor in that sense of authentic liberation you feel when you have genuinely forgiven, released all judgments, and are living as a fully empowered being. You may have to work hard for the initial feeling of inner liberation, and you may have to practice forgiveness off and on for the rest of your life, but the process becomes easier, second nature even, and the moments of true inner freedom become more and more frequent until you find that you are living in that state most of the time.

When we experience the freedom that comes from going through the three phases of this powerful process, the angry aspects of ourselves that once dictated our lives, our emotions, our responses and reactions, are released or transformed. We get to live "in the moment," free from the burdens of our past, free to stand in our authentic power, free to love and enjoy our lives!

## Why Forgive?

This book does not tell you that you *must* forgive for religious or moral reasons. I never urge you to embrace martyrdom, and I certainly don't encourage you to relinquish your self-respect or allow others to take advantage of you! Instead, you will experience the benefits of forgiving and how it leads to greater self-acceptance, improved relationships, and the opportunity to live the life you were meant to live. When the pain that is living inside your mind, heart and body is released, you become free to create a better life. You no longer have the need to blame the past, the world or even yourself for your misfortunes and suffering.

You may see your own pain and struggles mirrored in the stories shared in *The Real Meaning of the "F-Word."* You will come to understand that the suffering you are experiencing now, or have experienced in the past, is universal and that you are truly not alone. I show how the 3Fs Process has helped my clients stop living their lives defined by the wounds of the past. I outline how you can effectively employ these processes when you feel hurt, offended or betrayed by another person, or have done something to another that has made you feel ashamed and remorseful. Shame and resentment use up a lot of physical, mental and emotional energy. Just imagine what you could create with all of that energy if it were put toward productive manifestation instead!

Ultimately, *The Real Meaning of the "F-Word"* is about awakening to love. As the Sufi poet Rumi counseled, "Your task is not to seek for love, but merely to seek and find all the barriers within yourself that you have built against it." This book assists you in finding the barriers within, dissolving them, forgiving the past, and opening to authentic inner freedom. Forgiveness is the doorway to Freedom, which is the pathway to Love, the one thing we all want more than anything else.

*"Forgiveness is not an occasional act, it is a constant attitude."*
—Martin Luther King, Jr.

**Through the 3Fs Process, you will have the opportunity to** discover the answers to the following questions:

1. Is it possible for me to forgive Hitler and other people who have committed atrocities like genocide, murder, rape and abuse?

2. Can I really forgive if the person who hurt me isn't sorry?

3. Do anger, hurt and forgiveness have an impact on my physical health?

4. Does forgiveness require me to condone the behavior of others or "turn the other cheek" like a saint?

5. Does forgiveness require me to surrender my power?

6. What would it be like for me to live a life that isn't stuck in resentment?

7. How can I forgive when the person who abused me is the one who "was supposed" to love me?

8. Do I learn how to forgive (or not) from my family?

9. Why is it easier to forgive others than myself?

10. Can I really use a tragedy as a call to transform myself?

11. If I experience a small upset, do I still need to forgive?

*"True forgiveness is when you can say,*
*'Thank you for that experience.'"*
—Oprah Winfrey

## God in the Process

Part of the forgiveness process includes a reconciliation with God. Deep healing can occur when we ask for God's assistance. When we give our pain and judgment over to God, we are surrendering to a Higher Power while consciously opening our hearts to the healing power of forgiveness.

In the past, I occasionally felt uncomfortable speaking about God with certain clients. I thought my reluctance was a sign of respect for their beliefs and ideas, but at some point I knew there was something more. I was holding a judgment. I felt that leaving things in God's hands meant not taking responsibility, not "doing" what I was supposed to do. I thought it was the lazy way out.

After digging into the root cause of my judgments, I unearthed my limiting belief that because God had extremely serious and important business to attend to – wars, famine, global catastrophes – I didn't have the right to ask for help with my relatively petty concerns.

The Bible says in James 4:2-3, "You do not have because you do not ask God," and in Mark 7:7, "Ask and you will receive." I came to the realization that I was judging myself as undeserving, not important enough. Since that powerful moment, my relationship with God has changed dramatically. I started experiencing God inside of me instead of something separate from me. I knew that rather than asking God to fix things for me, I would ask God to give me the strength to overcome my challenges, to free myself from my patterns, and to be with me while I was going through the ups and downs of life.

I now ask my clients what their beliefs are and if they would be open to inviting God or a Higher Power to be a part of their healing process. Forgiveness, though a seemingly simple act, can be extremely difficult to accomplish at times. If we feel we cannot forgive on our own, asking God, Spirit, a Higher Power, or a Loving Presence to be present with us can give us the extra support we need to face our pain. The feeling that we do not have to be alone in our vulnerability can give us the strength to actually go through with the process of forgiving, which will ultimately bring about greater healing.

My client Joseph felt abandoned by God when he was raped as a young boy. The prisoner I worked with felt betrayed by God when his stepfather abused him, and Helena, the Holocaust survivor I counseled, firmly believed that God was not inside of the concentration camps.

It wasn't until each one of them was able to reconcile with God, in whatever way they experienced God, that they were able to fully accept, forgive and love themselves. Surrendering to God involves asking for the *"willingness-power"* (instead of the *"won't power"*) and the strength to cleanse ourselves in the purifying waters of unconditional forgiveness.

If an individual wants to participate in this powerful work and experience redemption, but doesn't believe in God, I ask them who their masters are or where their inspiration comes from, and I invite them to invoke the power of something bigger than themselves to assist them in the process.

*"To err is human, to forgive, divine."*
—Alexander Pope – An Essay on Criticism

The 3Fs Process encourages us to become centered in our hearts in order to fully experience the healing power of forgiveness. Now that you have chosen to embark on this transformational journey by reading this book and engaging in the forgiveness process, I invite you to center yourself in your heart by reading or reciting a poem, prayer or quote that inspires you.

I have always admired St. Francis for his inner strength and determination and have kept the "Prayer of St. Francis" inside my wallet for decades now. I include this prayer here in the hope that it provides you with a source of strength, love and inspiration. It reminds me that I reside in my loving when I allow myself to surrender to my own divine nature.

### *The Prayer of Saint Francis*

*Lord, make me an instrument of Your peace;*
*Where there is hatred, let me sow love;*
*Where there is injury, pardon;*
*Where there is discord, harmony;*
*Where there is error, truth;*
*Where there is doubt, faith;*
*Where there is despair, hope;*
*Where there is darkness, light;*
*And where there is sadness, joy.*
*O Divine Master, Grant that I may not so much seek*
*To be consoled as to console;*
*To be understood as to understand;*
*To be loved as to love.*
*For it is in giving that we receive;*
*It is in pardoning that we are pardoned;*
*And it is in dying that we are born to eternal life.*

✦ ✦ ✦

# CHAPTER ONE

# WHY FORGIVENESS IS THE KEY TO FREEDOM

*"Forgiveness does not change the past,*
*but it does enlarge the future."*
—Paul Boese

It was on a Monday morning in October 2010, a Monday that started like any other Monday. I was trying to decide which of my day-to-day issues I should handle first when I saw my husband waiting for me inside my meditation room. There were tears in his eyes.

"Please prepare yourself..." he said, "What I'm about to tell you will change our lives forever..."

***

Growing up, I was called "the forgiving one." Forgiveness had always come easily for me. But that fateful Monday, my ability to forgive was severely tested.

We had already been through a lot in the couple of years leading up to that day. My husband, a successful businessman, had suffered the financial consequences of a long lawsuit against his former partner who had embezzled funds from their business. As a result, nothing was left of the empire my husband had built for our family. After a long battle, in which he attempted to recover his assets, the only thing that remained was the bitterness that loss and betrayal had left in our hearts.

Those losses went beyond the economic. My husband's health also suffered as we worked on accepting the changes in our lifestyle and tried to rebuild our lives. I even found myself bargaining with God. "Please help us recover our money ... and our tranquility! If all of this trouble goes away, I'll forgive everything!" Of course, I knew that forgiveness had nothing to do with bargaining.

The strongest pillar in my life was my family – my husband and our only child, my amazing son, Seba. After all the trials we'd endured together, I felt more grateful than ever for the love and trust we shared. There was no way I could have fathomed the "perfect storm" that was about to completely upend my concept of "family." As my husband sat in my meditation room crying, I braced myself for what he was about to say.

"Almost 24 years ago, I had sex with someone else."

A thousand thoughts crossed my mind... *Why is it so important for him to tell me this right now? Out of the blue? This is more than the revelation of an old secret...* I sensed in my stomach that the punch was about to make contact, that my husband's infidelity wasn't the reason he was crying. All of this crossed my mind in the few seconds between his first confession and his next...

"And she had a son by me. He's now 23 years old."

My stomach contracted as I gasped. I had to replay his words in my head a couple of times to actually comprehend what he had just said to me. *My husband of almost 30 years betrayed me with another woman and fathered another child … with her… Our son isn't my husband's only son… Who is this man in front of me? Do I really know him?*

Before I could get out the question, "How do you know the boy is yours?" my husband said, "I had a DNA test done."

This news was quite a challenge for the "forgiving one." I had to ask myself if it was true that I was a forgiving person. Could I handle this?

I realized that what he was telling me could tear us apart … or it could be the path to heaven. As I wrote that sentence, I could almost hear your protests:

"Heaven? What are you talking about? Are you crazy?"

What I felt at that time was that this was an opportunity for me to move out of "hell" and closer to "heaven" by having the courage to face the pain and pull myself through and out of the rubble of the emotional debris to a place of greater spiritual maturity. I knew there was something more for me to look at than my husband's revelations, which were like images from a horror movie being projected over the movie of the life I'd thought I'd been living.

The light inside my heart wanted to expand beyond the hurt. I already knew how wonderful forgiveness could feel, and in this situation, as much as it tested my true nature, I realized that I, "the forgiving one," genuinely wanted to forgive.

I wasn't playing martyr, savior or saint. I wasn't nailing myself to the cross of suffering. I was experiencing redemption through the restorative, healing power of unconditional forgiveness. Even when the mind says there is no reason to forgive, the heart always knows there is. If that concept is puzzling to you, I promise that by the time you finish reading this book, you'll understand exactly what it means.

I continued to work through the process of forgiving my husband for his "transgression." The first step, of course, was working on accepting the changes that were taking place in our lives. One of the most challenging aspects of the revelation was accepting that my son's life would change as well. I so wanted to spare him any suffering. Just like I advise my clients, I had to move from the "F**k It!" phase through the "Full-Spectrum Forgiving" phase, in order to reach the final "Freedom" phase. In other words, I had to walk my talk!

As I was doing my own internal forgiveness work, I also continued to coach others through the 3Fs Process. Going through my own personal trial while coaching my clients through the challenges they shared with me helped me discover even deeper levels of healing and transformation than I thought possible.

## What is Forgiveness?

There are many misconceptions about forgiveness. Is it a religious duty? A moral obligation? Does it mean I'm condoning a hurtful, "wrong" act and letting the guilty party "off the hook"? Some people think they "should" forgive because it's the right thing to do. It's what their priest or pastor or rabbi tells them to do.

Forgiveness is actually a gift you give to yourself. It's an act of self-love. Forgiveness removes you from the "victim seat" and empowers you to move on with your life from a place of freedom, peace and health. You forgive for your own sake, not for anyone else's.

Forgiveness is not about reconciling, although sometimes it opens the door for genuine reconciliation. It doesn't mean that you have to forget what someone did to you, or say it was okay. It doesn't mean that you have to continue a relationship with the person you have forgiven. It doesn't mean that you give anyone permission to hurt you again. Pope John Paul II made headlines when he visited the man who had tried to kill him in prison. He was able to express compassion and forgiveness toward his perpetrator, but he certainly didn't set the man free.

Healthy boundaries are just that – healthy. Forgiving simply means that you come to a place where you can remember what happened without feeling the emotional hurt. It ceases to be in your "complaint repertoire" when talking with your confidants, and you no longer bring it up in arguments with the person who hurt you (if that person is still in your life). Many people falsely believe that forgiveness is a surrender of their power, but it's exactly the opposite. Forgiveness gives you *back* your power.

Perhaps you've heard these two expressions attributed to Buddha: "Holding onto anger is like taking poison and expecting the other person to die" and "Holding onto anger is like grasping a hot coal with the intent of throwing it at someone else, except you are the one who gets burned." I believe these sayings to be true. When you harbor resentment toward someone else – no matter what they did – it's you who are hurt.

Don't get me wrong, anger is a natural emotion. Repressing your anger, or feeling afraid of expressing it, is unhealthy. When you hold on to your anger, which you do whether you repress it or obsess over it, it controls your thoughts, feelings, behaviors, decisions and actions, and in essence, holds you prisoner. When you acknowledge your anger and choose to deal with it in a responsible and healthy manner, it becomes a path to healing that leads to forgiveness and ultimately transformation.

Forgiveness doesn't necessarily mean that you'll ever get an apology. You might; you might not. But true forgiveness allows you to move forward no matter what the other person does or does not do. If that individual isn't ready to grow, why should you hold yourself back from growth? It's self-defeating, isn't it?

Forgiveness means that you no longer hold others responsible for your own experiences. This is a difficult concept to grasp. My clients say to me, "But he really punched me!" or "She really did leave me at the altar! It's real! She was responsible for that, not me!"

Yes, I hear you. These things really happened. But we are all responsible for our reactions and feelings. We're responsible for the way we relate to the events in our lives and for the stories we tell ourselves about those experiences. When we don't change our story and reactions, we continue to recreate the past and live without hope for a different future. When we change our story, we have the opportunity to empower ourselves, to let go of the past, live in the present and move positively toward the future. We actually *manifest* a better tomorrow. Can you imagine who you would be without your story? Yes "that" story. The one that has defined you. I encourage you to start playing with the idea of letting it go...

Bear in mind while you navigate the chapters in this book, forgiveness is not an instantaneous process. It's an ongoing journey. Is it simple? Yes. Is it easy? No... not usually. That's because forgiveness is not a superficial process. It requires deep work, and it takes time for forgiveness to become genuine.

Forgiveness can happen instantaneously, but it can also be like peeling an onion, layer by layer, over a period of years. Lots of people say they have forgiven someone, but deep down, they still harbor resentment. And that resentment eats away at them. It affects the choices they make in their lives and the experiences they attract. It affects how they relate to other people. It alters their sense of self-worth, often causing them to unconsciously sabotage their goals and dreams. And they never even know they're doing it. They just know they aren't happy. They may think the same unpleasant things keep happening to them over and over for no apparent reason… but… there *is* a reason.

Forgiving doesn't mean that you'll never think an angry thought about the other person. We can't control the mind or the emotions. Many thoughts will come into your mind every day – flowing in and flowing out. What you *can* control is what you *hold* in your mind. You can learn to direct your thoughts and your emotions in healthy, expansive ways so that what you choose to *do* with those thoughts is productive and loving.

> *"We cannot choose our external circumstances,*
> *but we can always choose how we respond to them."*
> —Epictetus

## Forgive … and *Forget?*

You know the old adage, "forgive and forget." Well, "forgetting" can actually be a trap that causes you to suppress memories of the hurt. This causes a separation or dissociation inside you. One part within wants to express the pain and sadness, while the other part refuses to allow that expression.

This is what happened to my client, Joseph. A once healthy and mellow 60-year-old, he suddenly found himself so ill that he could barely speak or walk. He began to lose weight and ended up in the hospital. He appeared to be slowly dying, but the doctors couldn't figure out why. They assumed he had a terrible virus, but they couldn't identify it or understand the cause of his symptoms. Then they thought perhaps he had throat cancer. CAT scans, MRIs, and lab test after lab test could not produce a diagnosis.

In desperation, his wife suggested that he see me for coaching in the hope that he might recover his speaking voice. Initially, he had no intention of doing any deep spiritual or psychological work. But during our time together, the truth began to demand its say and rose up from deep within Joseph's psyche. In order to recover his voice, he had to speak his truth – a truth he had suppressed so completely that he had "forgotten" it.

This large man with salt and pepper hair, looked at me with a sad-eyed, childlike expression on his face, which oddly made him look even older than he was. In a hoarse, barely there voice that I had to struggle to hear, he asked, "Do you think painful memories from childhood can be healed?"

I knew something was coming to the surface, but I didn't yet know what it was. "Yes," I answered, "if the person is willing."

He began to shake like a leaf in a storm, and as he wept softly, he described a brutal gang rape that his cousin had endured when he was only eight years old. Joseph became so distraught while telling this story that he lost control of his bladder. A dark, wet stain spread across his lap as he uttered, "I couldn't save him, and you can't save him either!"

I knew he was talking about himself, not his cousin. The enormous shame he felt about not being able to defend himself against his attackers wouldn't allow him to admit that he, not his cousin, had been raped.

In vivid detail, Joseph continued to tell me the story of the attack that he kept claiming had happened to someone else. He spoke of the shame and the self-blame his cousin had felt. Finally, three days later, he was able to admit that he had been the innocent eight-year-old who had been raped. When he finally spoke the entire truth, his voice immediately began to recover. It was remarkable, but miracles can occur when we're ready to deal with our pain and move through it toward forgiveness.

Like many people who have been abused or deeply wounded, Joseph had unconsciously defined himself as wrong, shamed, weak, guilty and inferior because of what had happened to him when he was so young. Consciously, he believed that the best way to deal with it was to put it out of his mind and not look at it at all.

People often give you that advice, don't they? "Just forget about it, and move on." Yes, you want to move on, but "just forgetting about it" doesn't work because you don't really forget about it no matter how hard you try. Instead, you suppress it and split yourself into pieces inside in order to play the *game* of forgetting.

Joseph believed that because he survived the attack, he was okay. "It could have been worse," he told himself. For years, he thought he could function normally. He thought he had forgotten about the trauma, but the energy to suppress it took a toll on him. Eventually, images of the attack started coming to him as flashbacks.

In the process of turning away from his experience, Joseph resisted his pain and the part of himself that was damaged by the experience. Resistance became a survival mechanism. Since he believed that he survived because he resisted the pain, he believed unconsciously that his life depended on resisting. That concept became ingrained in his psyche so that he associated resisting with life.

He resisted happiness, he resisted sex, he resisted many good things because deep down inside he believed that he had to resist in order to survive. While he was in the throes of his illness, he even resisted the medications the doctors tried to give him. He couldn't swallow them properly. For him, resisting took many forms, and through our spiritual counseling work together, he began to recognize them.

After so many years of trying to hold his pain down, he just couldn't do it any longer. Even though resistance had been his survival, resisting life itself almost led him to an early death. In essence, he was killing himself in order to keep his secret – even from himself.

When Joseph began to unravel what was happening in his unconscious, he found monsters there – monsters that had often made appearances in his dreams. He had internalized his rapists as monsters; they lived inside him, attacking him over and over, until "they" almost killed him. He felt that they wouldn't allow him to have peace.

"I feel like I'm drowning," he explained to me. "Something bigger than me is soaking me in a deep ocean. I don't know who I am anymore. I'm a monster. I don't deserve to live."

Not only were there monsters trying to kill him from within, but in his mind, he had turned himself into a monster as well. This is the classic experience of self-blame when something painful happens to us.

"I will walk with you through the dark tunnel of your pain," I reassured Joseph. "I'll help you find the light. I know I can't feel this pain for you; only you can do that. But you aren't alone. By feeling this now and facing it from your adult perspective, you will be able to begin to heal. You'll be able to eventually accept what happened in the past and ultimately… yes… even forgive. Forgiveness is the final process of healing."

"Forgiveness?" he exclaimed.

"Yes, forgiveness – of everything that happened and of every single judgment you've made throughout the years. That's the road to liberation. You can't change the past, but you can change your perception of it. It will take some deep, painful work, but the good news is that the pain will be temporary. If you hold on to it and don't ever let it go, the pain will continue forever. If you walk through it, you will come to a point when you're ready and willing to forgive. It will be organic, and it will feel like a relief. Trust me, I've been there, and I've seen it many times."

Joseph began to understand that he couldn't pretend the pain away anymore – not if he wanted to live. It took us several months of working together to uncover the many beliefs, emotions, behaviors and attitudes that had been shaped by that violent childhood experience.

Through a deep process of forgiveness – forgiveness of his perpetrators, as well as himself – he was able to get better both physically and emotionally. You may be wondering why he had to forgive himself. It is important to understand that Joseph judged himself as a result of his experience. In order for him to identify and release his misperceptions, and see himself as the gentle, powerful, courageous man he really was, he needed to forgive the judgments he held against himself.

He was eventually able to recognize that what had happened to him was not his fault. When he finally brought his adult consciousness to the beliefs he had formed as an eight-year-old – beliefs he had never challenged in his adulthood because he had never been aware of them – the healing process truly began.

Throughout his life, Joseph had believed on some level that what had happened to him when he was eight had made him less of a man. As a result, he'd spent his entire life trying to prove his manhood to himself and others. He would attract experiences that caused him to once again feel he was not a real man.

These experiences were verifications of what he believed about himself. He thought that if he could get certain things – more money or the attention of other women besides his wife – they would help him feel powerful. The truth was, the only thing that could help him feel like a man was an inner state of empowerment.

Joseph had to acknowledge and accept the pain, upset, hurt and anger he felt. He had to go through the F**k It! phase and the release of judgments in the Full-Spectrum Forgiving phase. If he had tried to force himself to forgive too quickly – before the judgments had genuinely been relinquished on a deep level – he would not have experienced true forgiveness or healing. Whatever relief he might have felt or experienced would have been fleeting and superficial. The struggle would have bubbled up again, and he might even have become dreadfully ill a second time.

I fully believe that it was our focus on forgiveness that accounted for the speed of Joseph's progress. Within six months, all his physical symptoms were resolved. He could walk again, he could speak normally and he started to put on weight. He wasn't ill anymore. But let me say here that although he was cured of his physical ailments, he was still not fully healed. Even though the work he'd done on the emotional and mental levels was beneficial to his physical condition, he still had more deep inner healing to experience.

One day in my office, Joseph carefully examined the words – representing emotions and emotional states – I have printed on large individual pieces of paper posted on my bulletin board. I use the words with my clients to trigger responses. Joseph unpinned three of the papers from my board: LAUGHTER, PEACE and HAPPINESS.

He smiled gently at me and said after staring at the words: "I've been looking at your papers with these words printed on them for a long time now, but this is the first time I've made eye contact with them." So, in a sense, if we want to "make eye contact," as Joseph said, with peace, genuine laughter, authenticity and joy, we also need to make "eye contact" with forgiveness.

Joseph and I continued to work together, and eventually he started feeling free. That newfound freedom allowed him to express love and enjoy himself. He gave himself permission to live and laugh. He no longer felt split within himself or separated from others. He was free to relate to life from his heart, *not from his hurt*. What's more, he had the tools for dealing with the old feelings whenever they came to the surface again. If he felt unworthy, he had a compass to guide himself back to freedom and equilibrium.

*"If we say that monsters [people who do terrible evil] are beyond forgiving, we give them a power they should never have ... they are given the power to keep their evil alive in the hearts of those who suffered most. We give them power to condemn their victims to live forever with the hurting memory of their painful pasts. We give the monsters the last word."*
—Lewis B. Smedes

## The "Pain Code"

When we experience a hurt, it's like a "pain code" that becomes imprinted on the software inside of us. The only way to update the software is to release the anger and repressed memories, and then work on accepting and forgiving without rationalizing. When Joseph forgave the monsters, they no longer occupied the space inside of him where they had lived for so long. He no longer needed to identify with the hurt and suffering.

*"In order to take the front seat in your own life,
you have to stop identifying yourself as a victim."*

When Joseph forgave his rapists, it wasn't because they "deserved" forgiveness. At first, he wanted a reason to forgive them, but eventually he was able to forgive without the need to justify his forgiveness. He forgave them for *himself*, not for them.

When we feel we can't forgive someone unless and until they *earn* that forgiveness, we're coming from a place of ego, and we might have to wait forever. Authentic forgiveness is *unconditional*. You don't need a *reason* to forgive, other than your own need for inner peace and well-being. Remember that condoning and forgiving are two different things!

*"Sincere forgiveness isn't colored with expectations that the other
person apologizes or changes. Don't worry whether or not they finally
understand you. Love them and release them. Life feeds back truth
to people in its own way and time."*
—Sara Paddison

We often equate forgiveness with weakness, but as you can see from Joseph's story, forgiving yourself or someone else takes tremendous courage. In order to truly forgive, you must face what happened, let go of the hurt from an authentic place, accept the past, surrender to unconditional forgiveness, and move on with your life. As Mahatma Gandhi said, "The weak can never forgive. Forgiveness is the attribute of the strong."

## The Cycle of Dehumanization

Without forgiveness, there is no end to violence. Another man I have worked with is serving a life sentence for killing his fiancée because he thought she was cheating on him. After his fatal outburst of rage, he was overwhelmed with guilt and remorse and turned himself in.

"What if *I'm* the monster?" he asked me. "I'm the one who caused suffering to others. I took the life of a woman!"

*Maybe it's sometimes easier to be the victim than the perpetrator,* I thought. *At least the victim is seen as the good guy.*

Like Joseph, this man, Johnny, had been raped as a child. The unresolved anger he carried inside him exploded in a moment of unspeakable violence. As a result of losing control in that way, he struggled to see himself as human, and he didn't consider himself worthy of forgiveness or love. That was where our work began.

You may find it hard to think of Johnny as worthy of forgiveness, which is exactly how he felt about himself. I understand this, but when we don't forgive, we continue a cycle of dehumanization that has no end. Because Johnny hadn't forgiven his perpetrator, his anger was never released. It remained bottled up inside of him until he became a perpetrator himself.

Anger gives birth to more anger that gives birth to more anger and more and more from generation to generation to generation. Through this cycle, people learn to hate, unless and until the cycle is interrupted, and somehow love is introduced in its place.

As Nelson Mandela said, "No one is born hating another person because of the color of his skin or his background or his religion. People must learn to hate, and if they can learn to hate, they can be taught to love, for love comes more naturally to the human heart than its opposite."

As I said, forgiveness is not something we do because people deserve it. Forgiveness is not a prize for good behavior or for feeling "enough" remorse. As you will understand more fully after reading the chapters that follow, true forgiveness requires that we let go of judgments against ourselves as well as others. If we demand that someone deserve our forgiveness, we are still holding on to those judgments. Only when we are able to forgive – even people and acts we believe are unforgivable – can we be free.

In 2013, I had the extraordinary opportunity to meet Patrick Chamusso at a conference in Santa Monica, California. Before meeting him, we watched the film, *Catch a Fire*, in which Chamusso's fight against Apartheid in South Africa was depicted. He had been a prisoner at the same time and in the same prison on Robben Island as Nelson Mandela; it was during this period that the two men became close.

During the conference, Chamusso spoke about his horrific experiences. The prison personnel actually injected him with the HIV virus as a form of torture. It's hard to imagine such cruelty, isn't it? While he was behind bars, all he could think about was getting out and killing the people who had done those horrible things to him. Then he spoke to Mandela, who advised him to forgive.

Of course, Chamusso had work to do before he could truly let go and forgive, but Mandela helped him to realize that killing his perpetrators would only make his own life worse. It would not help him feel better. In fact, he would without a doubt end up right back in prison where they could torture him further.

As both Johnny and Chamusso discovered, revenge doesn't change the past, and it doesn't soothe the pain. Instead, an "eye for an eye" mentality keeps you chained to your hatred and pain. Whether your prison is literal like Johnny's and Chamusso's or figurative like Joseph's, refusing to forgive keeps you locked up.

*"To forgive is to set a prisoner free*
*and discover that the prisoner was you."*
—Lewis B. Smedes

If people like Joseph, Patrick Chamusso, Nelson Mandela and some of my other clients, like Helena, a Holocaust survivor, can forgive, so can you. And you can forgive the smaller painful events in your life, too. Sometimes, a careless comment from someone can trigger you and cause a great deal of hurt. Those events are not to be trivialized. Your feelings about them are valid and demand expression, and ultimately your forgiveness.

## Forgiveness Quiz

How do you know if you need to do forgiveness work? Take this quiz to find out. You can take it again after you have finished the book and worked through the 3Fs process so that you can compare your results and see your progress.

For each statement, decide if you strongly agree, agree somewhat, feel undecided, disagree somewhat, or strongly disagree. Then, by each statement, write the corresponding number of points for your answer. For example, if you "agree somewhat" with a statement, your points for that statement would be "4."

| | |
|---|---|
| Strongly Agree | 5 points |
| Agree Somewhat | 4 points |
| Undecided | 0 points |
| Disagree Somewhat | 2 points |
| Strongly Disagree | 1 point |

| Statement | Score |
|---|---|
| 1. If I forgive someone who hurt me, it's like giving them permission to do it again. | |
| 2. If I forgive someone, it means I should reconcile with them. | |
| 3. I tend to complain a lot. | |
| 4. I have to understand why someone did something wrong in order to consider forgiving them. | |
| 5. I tend to live in the past. | |
| 6. I can forgive, but I never forget. | |
| 7. If I forgive myself for my errors, I am not responsible for my actions. | |
| 8. My future is determined by what happened in my past. | |
| 9. I don't believe in second chances. | |
| 10. The only way someone will understand how I feel is to suffer the same pain. | |
| 11. Revenge is the path to justice. | |
| 12. I believe forgiveness is important, but it is not the door to happiness. | |
| 13. Only saints can forgive atrocities, and I'm certainly not a saint. | |
| 14. People who say they are forgiving are like martyrs. | |
| 15. Although I forgive people who hurt me, I still harbor a bit of anger toward them. | |

| | |
|---|---|
| 16. I judge people harshly. | |
| 17. I believe there is truth in the saying, "revenge is sweet." | |
| 18. I cannot forgive myself for something I have done if the person I hurt doesn't forgive me. | |
| 19. I would never be able to experience closure with someone who passed away. | |
| 20. If someone hurts me, sooner or later they will pay for it. | |
| 21. My family is slow to forgive, so that is the way things should be. It runs in the family. | |
| 22. If someone hurts the people I love, they hurt me forever. | |
| 23. If I release my anger, it means I have condoned what the other person did. | |
| 24. Some people just don't deserve forgiveness. | |
| 25. I can forgive the person who wronged me if they ask for forgiveness and shows remorse. | |
| ADD UP YOUR TOTAL TO GET YOUR SCORE | TOTAL: |

## *If your score is between 26 and 46:*

You are a forgiving person. Either it comes naturally to you, or you have learned the power of forgiveness, and you apply it to your life. You possess the quality of compassion. It is important that you keep up your good work and use the forgiveness tools in every small challenge you face in life. Forgiveness will also help you release issues related to your health.

### *If your score is between 47 and 90:*

You believe in the power of forgiveness. You work through the process, and you are eager to improve your emotional and physical health. You possess the quality of compassion, and you are willing to extend it toward yourself and others. Still, there are times when you find forgiveness to be very challenging. You would benefit from working through the 3Fs so that you don't hide from your emotions.

### *If your score is between 91 and 130:*

You would definitely benefit from immersing yourself in the 3Fs process. You are still attached to the past and your old hurts. But don't feel discouraged! Your emotional, mental and physical health will improve if you are willing to work on forgiveness. It can be learned; the choice is yours. If you want to live a fulfilling life, start using the tools provided in this book to open your life to new possibilities.

***

How did you do? Whatever your score, remember what a good friend of mine says: "We will be doing forgiveness work until the last breath." As I said, forgiveness is simple, but it isn't always easy.

Throughout these pages, you will read more about my personal story and more about my clients, all of whom have gone through the 3Fs process. You will learn how you too can experience the same level of profound healing that I, Joseph, Johnny and many others have experienced.

Even if you have found forgiveness impossible so far in your life, you *can* learn to forgive. It's your choice… You can continue to blame yourself, your life circumstances and others, or you can work through the F**k It! phase to release your emotional pain so that you can move on to the Full-Spectrum Forgiving phase, and then on to the Freedom phase and your own liberation!

*"When we are willing to experience the power of forgiveness, we are close to our own divinity, to the essence of love – closer to who we really are."*

✦ ✦ ✦

CHAPTER TWO

# THE 3Fs PROCESS

*If we really want to love, we must learn how to forgive.*
—Mother Teresa

The 3Fs Process is outlined here at the very beginning of the book in order to introduce the concepts and language before you delve into the remainder of the book. Chapters Three through Nine take you more deeply into the concepts underlying the Process and explain the benefits of doing forgiveness work through examples and stories.

My hope is that all of your questions about how and why this Process works will be answered by the time you get to the end of Chapter Nine. You may want to try the exercises in this chapter right away, or you may wish to read the entire book before you come back to this Process.

\*\*\*

My husband and I chose to spend healing time in nature after we learned that he had another son, so we decided to visit the magical

Mariposa Grove of Giant Sequoias in California's Yosemite National Park. While there, I learned that the most ancient sequoias are about 3,000 years old, and the miracle that keeps them alive for so long is the elemental power of fire. The power of fire... amazing, right?

When forest fires are naturally ignited (usually by lightning) they burn through the sequoia forests and clear everything that threatens the trees. If it weren't for the fires, the sequoias would not have enough sunlight to grow. The fires open a space for birth and transformation, and in fact, without the heat the fires generate, the sequoias cannot release their seeds. The sequoias also have an amazing survive mechanism that allows them to self-heal and keep growing when injured.

As John Muir said about the sequoia forests: "By forces seemingly antagonistic and destructive, nature accomplishes her benefiting – designs now a flood of fire, now a flood of ice... and again in the fullness of time an outburst of organic life..."

We can apply these analogies to our own lives: the growth cycle of the sequoias reflects our own psychological and spiritual growth cycles of clearing and transformation. How often in our lives do we experience our relationships, work and plans metaphorically going up in flames? Do we, like the giant sequoias, have to "go through the fire" to experience the clearing necessary to grow? Can experiencing "heat" – distress, anger, suffering, grief – provide us with the opportunity to release the seeds that create new birth? As the sequoias do, can we go from hurt to healing? Can we experience a clearing after the fire has burned out? Can we thrive in spite of our scars?

It is challenging to focus on potential opportunities that may come about as a result of the "clearing" that occurs after a metaphorical fire has blown through our life, especially when we are in the middle of the conflagration. But being alert to possibility opens the door to transformation. Each of us will experience difficult times and challenging passages; if we can consider those crucial moments as opportunities for releasing seeds of hope, we can experience forward movement.

When we find ourselves going through the burning fire of anger, loss and pain, how do we experience rebirth? How do we let go of the ego's desire to get revenge, or the tendency to succumb to resentment, or see ourselves as failures? How do we release the seeds of our own rebirth? The ability to emerge from the fire reborn comes through the blessing of forgiveness.

How do we shift into the soul level where we can access forgiveness? Through the exercises presented in this chapter you will learn to release limiting thoughts and fears, transform resistance and connect to your soul essence. From there, through forgiveness, you will be able to expand in consciousness and finally experience the true freedom of self-acceptance and self-love.

What is the difference between these three steps and tons of other forgiveness exercises? It is one thing to read and "know" about forgiveness, but it is a different thing to experience it. That is the reason the 3Fs Process encourages you to submerge in the deep work of forgiveness with an open mind and open heart, so the knowledge becomes the wisdom of your heart and soul.

\*\*\*

The first phase of the 3Fs Process offers you the possibility of truly feeling your feelings, of fully expressing them, so you empty the "bowl" that can then be filled with love. The "bowl" refers to a Buddhist allegory. If you ask for rice with a bowl that is already full, you cannot receive anything. You have to empty the bowl in order to receive. In the same way, we need to empty our mind or "bowl," so our heart can receive.

Have you noticed that if someone hurts you and then apologizes, sometimes it is not enough? You forgive, but now and then you encounter similar situations that activate your hurt feelings all over again. If receiving or granting forgiveness doesn't wash away the suffering or pain completely, what does? The second phase of the 3Fs Process guides you through exercises that encourage you to clear all of your judgments. It is only then that the "bowl," which once contained toxic hurt feelings and thoughts, is empty and can receive or be filled up with compassion, love and peace.

Our emotions are "locked in" when we associate a judgment with a particular emotion. Every time an emotion we perceive to be negative is triggered, our "pain system" gets activated. Through practical exercises, the three phases of this process assist you in removing the judgments and liberating the emotions that are "locked in." The final phase of the 3Fs Process opens the door to real freedom, so you are able to maintain and cultivate lasting inner peace. The bowl that is emptied will be replenished through this Forgiveness Process.

## The Three Phases

Path to Awakening

3. Freedom

1. F**k It! ⟶ 2. Full-Spectrum Forgiving

34

## 1. Phase One: F**k It!

In this phase, we say to *ourselves*: "What the f**k just happened to me? F**k this! F**k him! How dare he do that to me?!" This is an important, normal, human phase that we must experience in order to acknowledge and validate the shock and the anger we feel about being hurt. Repressing our anger and pain is as unhealthy as lashing out at the perceived perpetrator of our pain. In this phase, we honor our hurt and dare to go into the dark places within to embrace the pain so that we may release and transform it.

In this phase, we acknowledge our tendency to blame – others, as well as ourselves. We learn to unearth our wounds and express anger in a healthy way. Only then can the anger and hurt be transformed. Only then can we move to phase two – The Full-Spectrum Forgiving phase. Many people want to jump from the F**k It! phase to the final or Freedom phase, but that never works. If we gloss over the F**k It! phase and command ourselves to "just get over it" or "just forgive, forget and move on," we suppress our true feelings and end up attracting new circumstances that will bring the same hurts back to the surface again. The names in the story may change, but the resentment will be all too familiar.

## 2. Phase Two: Full-Spectrum Forgiving

This is the heart of the 3Fs Process. Full-Spectrum Forgiving means forgiving everyone – yourself as well as others. In this phase, we begin to disengage from the anger and hurt, as we bring into our awareness our beliefs and misconceptions, some of which were formed as a result of our negative experiences. We begin to realize that the stories in our heads are only stories... and that we can detach from and ultimately let go of these dramas that have held us hostage.

Letting go requires unearthing and acknowledging judgments we've been holding against ourselves and others. Only when we bring these judgments into our awareness do we have the power to choose to reevaluate their relevance in our lives. Once this baggage has been released, it's possible to see our hurts from a different perspective. The mind might tell you that there is no good reason to forgive, but the heart will awaken you to the possibility.

When all your judgments have been released and transformed, the actual moment of forgiveness can be quick, like the moment when a key finally unlocks a stuck door. Sometimes, though, forgiveness will happen in small bits and pieces over a period of time. We cannot surrender to forgiveness until we are ready to do it from an authentic, deeply felt place.

By the end of the book, you will be better able to identify the genuine unfolding of the Full-Spectrum Forgiving phase of the Process. You will also learn that while genuine reconciliation may be part of the process, forgiveness is ultimately for your transformation, health and well-being.

## 3. *Phase Three: Freedom*

The liberation you feel when you experience true forgiveness can be life-changing. Freedom – true inner freedom – becomes a way of life. As the prison inmates I've worked with have discovered, inner freedom can be experienced even in the confines of a prison. We know we're free from the past when we can remember an old hurt without feeling angry, anxious or agitated. That is when we know the chains around our hearts have been cut.

In this phase we learn to have greater awareness of our judgments so that we can disengage from them. As a result, we begin to be who we really are. We are not our stories anymore, we are no longer our pain and no longer the victim or the perpetrator. As author, medical intuitive and mystic Caroline Myss says: "What we don't forgive becomes a part of us."

We experience inner freedom, because those "parts" that no longer serve us have dissolved. This is a result of the work we have done in the F\*\*k It! phase, where we released the energy of our emotions, and in the Full-Spectrum Forgiving phase, where we identified and transformed through forgiveness our judgments against ourselves, others and God.

## Benefits of the 3Fs Process

* Empowers us to take personal responsibility for our upsets, dramas and crises, so we can heal and move on – even if we've been the victim of a crime.
* Assists us in healing anything that disturbs our inner peace.
* Serves us in developing a habit of using everything for our healing, learning and growth.
* Builds a sense of confidence and self-worth, knowing we have the inner strength to heal whatever upset or issue we might encounter in life.
* Gives us the ability to respond (response-ability), rather than react.
* Stops the wheel of continuous suffering.
* Gives us the opportunity to experience the value of healing the hurt inside, and gives us the skills to heal all of our issues.
* Gives us a sense of calm – an inner freedom – that provides us with the opportunity to live life more fully.
* Empowers us to be who we really are – who we are meant to be.

It is important to be clear about the benefits we will experience when we submerge ourselves in this work. We must see the benefits as the "light at the end of the tunnel," so when we have doubts or feel we want to quit, we can inspire and encourage ourselves with the brilliant vision of what lies ahead…

*"Do not assume that divine guidance flows only when you are in need of help. Guidance continues to flow whether or not you have problems. It transcends problems, heartbreaks, and traumas, flowing through dreams and illuminations. Whether guidance comes during times of tranquility or trauma, however, it is up to you to have the courage to acknowledge it"*
—Caroline Myss

## Preparing for the 3Fs Process

In order to prepare to work the 3Fs Process, check in with yourself to make sure you're willing. If you sense inner resistance to doing the work, ask yourself if you think you can continue in spite of the resistance. Acknowledge that part of the process is moving through the resistance.

If you feel you cannot move through your feelings of resistance on your own, but are nonetheless interested in transforming and/or releasing your pain, this may be an indication that working with a counselor, therapist or coach will be the most beneficial and supportive path for you at this moment. On the other hand, give it a try… remember, you have nothing to lose, and a lot to gain!

\*\*\*

Before you begin, create a private sanctuary in your home – a sacred space where you feel comfortable releasing feelings. You can create an altar using objects that are sacred to you – stones, statues, artwork, candles, mirrors, leaves, flowers and anything that inspires, uplifts and/or comforts you. You can use incense, essential oils and flowers to infuse your space with the scents you love.

You can play soft, sacred or classical music or use singing bowls, drums, small gongs or any other instrument, that when played, gives you a sense of peace and comfort. You can place beautiful pillows or carpets around your altar to sit or lie on. This is your space, so you can use anything that helps you feel safe and peaceful inside. Once you have created this place of solace, you can use it at any time to engage in your forgiveness work.

If you do not have the space in your home to create an actual sanctuary, or if you do not wish to create one, it is possible to create that space inside yourself. The truth is that you always carry your own sanctuary within, whether you use it or not. You can find this safe and peaceful "space" by simply sitting somewhere quiet and private. As you sit, close your eyes and focus on your heart center by placing one or both hands over your heart. Breathe slowly, gently and consciously, while training your mind's eye on anything that gives you a feeling of safety and inner peace.

You might visualize a private beach, a quiet forest trail, your beloved pet, or even an object like a piece of art you love. You might imagine being held by someone you love and trust, perhaps even an Angel, a Spirit Guide or Ascended Master. Something I love to imagine when I'm preparing myself to do forgiveness work is the feeling of floating in warm blue water. That sensation helps me become centered, relaxed and ready to do the work.

Before you begin the 3Fs Process, even if your emotions are boiling over, I recommend sitting in a comfortable position in your sanctuary, or accessing the "sanctuary within," and doing a short meditation during which you focus your energy and attention on an intention for your forgiveness session.

Intentions are a way to create your reality… actually a way to "co-create" your reality. By stating your positive decision to move in a certain direction, Spirit (God, your Higher Self, the Universe, or whatever label feels most comfortable for you) hears your determination and joins forces with you in order to assist you in realizing your goals, dreams and heartfelt desires. For example, you might state: "My intention is to let go of (name the circumstance that upset you or the person who hurt you), and any pain associated with that situation, and instead to experience peace for the highest good of all concerned."

Please note that "setting an intention" has a different energy than "trying to make a change." We empower our intention by focusing our attention. Whatever we focus our attention on tends to expand, so focusing our attention on our intention strengthens our ability to manifest what we genuinely want.

Through meditation, we can experience ourselves beyond whatever is going on in our lives. I use a simple breathing technique to get into a meditative state – it helps me be present with myself and calm any inner turbulence I may be experiencing.

Close your eyes and inhale deeply as you count slowly to four. Consciously feel the air flow into your lungs and fill your belly. You may want to put a hand over your belly so you can feel the air as it fills your body. Visualize the fresh air coming into your body and invigorating your cells. Exhale to the count of eight. Do this breathing exercise/meditation for five minutes, or more if you like. After you have finished meditating, the state you are now in is your reference point for internal equilibrium. Meditation quiets your thoughts and feelings, which clears a space inside your mind and heart for the forgiveness process.

This is the time, after meditating and before engaging in the forgiveness process, to write down the intention you focused on during your meditation and place it on your altar or post it where you can see it. After you have set your intention, create an "Ideal Scene" in your mind through visualization. This powerful exercise can help you focus on how you *want* to feel and live, instead of on your pain.

When you begin your process by visualizing the outcome you'd like to experience, you set yourself up for success. An Ideal Scene is simply the scenario you'd like to be experiencing, rather than the one you are currently experiencing. If, for instance, you have felt betrayed by your spouse and are working to forgive him/her, you may want to visualize a scenario in which the two of you are holding hands while happily strolling together in a beautiful garden.

In this scene, you will of course want to imagine how you feel… and obviously, you will want to be feeling happy, at peace and in love! This does not have to be an elaborate scenario or one that you write down (though you may choose to do so), but you will want to see it clearly and really feel the happiness and joy you desire. Sit with this image/feeling for a few minutes, until you begin to relax into it.

You don't need to question your Ideal Scene. Give yourself permission to imagine your desired outcome. When you start questioning yourself during this preparation phase, there is a possibility that you could get stuck in resistance, focusing on the struggle rather than the desired outcome. Breathe, reread your intention, place your hands on your heart center, and to the best of your ability focus on your vision. See it and feel it for as long as it takes to make it seem real.

If this feels impossible, just do your best! Lovingly support yourself as you go through this process. Acknowledge to yourself that you are brave to be facing your pain, and allow yourself to move on to the first phase of the forgiveness process even if you are not sure that you actually believe your Ideal Scene. The more you work this process, the closer you will get to your desired outcome. Eventually you will achieve your goal of experiencing inner peace and freedom!

## Working with the 3-F's Process

### F**K IT!

In this phase, you identify the hurt, although you don't have to name it yet. This works when you feel like a victim of someone else's actions or words, as well as when you feel guilt or shame for your own errors and mistakes.

So how do you start moving through the F**k It! phase? You have already done your meditation and visualization, so you are ready to dive deep into your pain. The reason we have to dive into our pain is that when we don't know how to deal with pain – when we suppress it, ignore it, or deny it – we experience toxicity.

The emotions we have stuffed down begin to fester, and eventually become toxic for us and others in our energy field. "Toxic" emotions frequently overflow (mostly unintentionally) onto those around us. Even though we think we are controlling our emotions by sitting on them, the truth is that they are controlling us; whatever we do or don't do, express or don't express, is "manipulated" by those internal feelings, or more accurately, by what they become the more they are avoided and denied.

When we experience sadness, anger, worry, frustration, or any other negative emotion, the upset is often just a "trigger" that reenergizes an older hurt or unresolved issue that is still lodged in our unconscious. When we are able to recognize that our emotional reaction to the person or circumstance that has upset us may have deeper roots, we can choose to use that upset as an opportunity for growth and healing at a deeper level.

It is not easy to deal with painful emotions head-on. When we are in the middle of the experience, we don't generally think about the learning opportunity available to us or the potential for growth and expansion in consciousness before us; we are just hurt and angry.

I know you'd prefer to avoid emotional pain and suffering (painful feelings that don't end), but pain is a normal part of life and is unavoidable. However, suffering is not. The good news is that we can learn how to deal with pain so that we don't have to suffer. Being courageous and choosing to make conscious decisions are the qualities that help us move through the pain of the F**k It! phase.

We have choices. We can live permanently in the F**k It! phase, where everything in our lives ends up being painful, or we can learn to accept and process our feelings, and eventually move on. When we live permanently in this state, we are obsessed with our thoughts; we believe we are the emotions we feel. When we get stuck in this stage, we victimize ourselves.

The victim mentality allows you to reject personal responsibility. You see yourself as a victim in every situation, which often leads to blaming everyone and everything for your life circumstances. By refusing to recognize, accept and process our emotions, we begin to feel drained, exhausted and paralyzed, which will eventually affect our physical health. Toxic emotions will lead to a toxic body.

If we don't deal with our pain when it occurs, it will resurface later on in our lives. It can come in different guises such as: apathy, depression, hostility, haughtiness, arrogance, sarcasm, anxiety, or in the form of judgmental attitudes, prejudices and rationalizations. Through the processes in this book, you can learn how to recognize painful emotions and the thoughts associated with them, and with practice, you can learn to how to effectively "metabolize" them by experiencing and releasing the pain, which will prevent suffering.

When our minds know, we call it knowledge; when our hearts know, it is wisdom. Through these exercises, you will be able to travel from your mind into your heart. You may do one of them or all of them. When I work with my clients, I have them do all the exercises in the order in which they are presented below. I have found that by following this order, they move through the 3Fs Process more gracefully and feel complete by the time they finish the last exercise.

Take as much time as you need. You are learning the art of letting go, which might take time. Remember, healing is a process, not an event.

## F**k It! – Exercise 1
### Identifying Your Emotions – Awareness

Are you angry? Frustrated? Are you upset, but not sure what it is you actually feel? Sit comfortably, close your eyes and practice your meditation breathing for a moment. Try to identify the emotion by locating it physically. In other words, where inside your body do you feel it? Do you feel like you're being strangled or punched in the stomach? Does your head feel like it's in a vise? Does your heart feel like it's being stabbed? Bring your awareness to the "physical" pain.

This process not only helps us identify our emotions, but we learn to listen to the various signals our bodies give us.

You don't need to do anything; just sit with the sensations you're experiencing. Accept them. Don't judge them. Tell yourself that it's okay to feel. You do not need to rationalize, justify or explain. Don't hide from your feelings, just BE with them. You can wrap your arms around yourself to give yourself support while you feel the pain in your body.

You might feel compassion, or you might feel sadness or rage. Love yourself through it all. You are simply experiencing the feelings and the emotions now. You cannot let go of what you don't recognize. This is not about what anyone did to you; this is about you and your feelings. If images of others come up, just acknowledge them and let them go.

This process can be uncomfortable, so it's important to know that you're not the feelings; they're just sensations that you happen to be experiencing. Taking responsibility doesn't mean you are guilty. It just means you are recognizing that these are YOUR feelings regarding a painful experience.

Some of the sensations you are feeling may be associated with memories of older hurts in addition to whatever triggered your current upset. Your body is responding to the emotions with muscle contractions, spasms, aches and tears, and when you take responsibility for YOUR feelings, you empower yourself to let them go.

## F**k It! – Exercise 2
### Being the Neutral Observer – Detachment

For the next few minutes, think in detail about what happened to you. Every detail of what happened. Where were you? What was

45

said or implied? Detach from the experience by imagining that you are just reporting it. Just "watch" it. If you become too involved, start again… you can do it. You are not what happened, you are not the victim, you are not the abuser. You are just watching the events.

The purpose of this exercise is to see things as a neutral observer of what happened. In the big scheme of life, even if what happened to you was deeply traumatic, it doesn't have to define your whole life. It is difficult but not impossible. Imagine being on top of a mountain; look from that perspective and ask yourself: "Who would I be without these feelings? How would I experience life without the thoughts I have about this situation? How do I feel when I see myself as a neutral observer?"

## F**k It! – Exercise 3
## Describing Your Feelings – Clarity

Now identify exactly what you are feeling. Name the feeling(s). Use specific words to describe your feeling(s), as well as words/phrases that help you define/describe your experience. Be as precise as you can. The words/phrases that come up may surprise you; your feelings may not be what you originally thought they were. The words/phrases that come to you may be related to other times when you experienced similar feelings. Be open.

If the phrase, "I feel angry," comes forward for you, repeat, "I feel angry *because*…" several times to yourself. Eventually, you will be able to complete the phrase with something like: "I feel angry because I feel insulted. I feel I don't matter. I feel unappreciated. I feel betrayed. I feel I have been treated unfairly. I don't deserve this. He/she doesn't deserve my love! Life is unfair! I hate him/her/them! They will pay for what they've done to me!"

## *F**k It! – Exercise 4*
## *Releasing Your Feelings – Relief*

Now is the time to express those feelings. Since you have located the emotions in your physical body, put your hands and your focus on those places and say or scream out loud: "It hurts here!" and/or anything else that comes up for you. Scream, cry, punch a pillow (with the intention of letting the hurt energy go, not with the intention of getting even or hurting the person who hurt you).

You need to move the energy. After you have expressed your feelings, if you still feel the energy of your emotions running through your body, you can do several different things to continue to release the energy. Walk briskly, stomp around, run or take a hike, dance freely to music that expresses how you feel, do calisthenics, swim, work out or punch a punching bag. Anything that does not harm you or anyone else, but that helps you move and release the stuck energy.

## *F**k It! – Exercise 5*
## *Writing Your Emotions – Liberation*

After you have worked some of your emotional energy out through expression and movement, you can choose to continue processing your emotions by doing "Free Form Writing." For this exercise, you'll want to light a candle, have a spiral notebook or several pieces of loose paper and a pen nearby (I don't recommend doing this on a computer). This is material that you will NOT keep. In fact, you will not reread anything you write, and you certainly won't send it to the person who hurt you. This is just for you – a safe place for you to get your feelings out.

Begin writing about the hurt. What do you feel? Write whatever thoughts come into your mind. You do not have to be clear or concise.

You do not have to write neatly. You do not have to write in complete sentences or pay attention to spelling, grammar or punctuation. In fact, if you can't get words out, you are free to scrawl, scribble and scratch your feelings into the notebook. You might find yourself writing, "I feel stupid. I don't know what I feel. I hate doing this." That's fine. But keep writing, even if you write, "I hate this!" over and over again. Encourage yourself to move through your resistance, so that you eventually find yourself connecting with your feelings.

Once you have made this connection, imagine that you are writing or speaking (even though this is a "writing" exercise, it's fine for you to speak out loud at this point if it is a more effective way for you to get your feelings out) directly to the person who "wronged" you or the person you feel you "wronged." Either write the person a letter (which you won't send), or imagine that the individual is there while you say or shout out loud what you'd like them to hear.

If it helps, choose an object to represent the person, such as a chair, a stuffed animal or doll, a stone, statue, etc. Write or say/shout everything you'd like to express. Come from as deep a truth within yourself as possible. You don't have to worry about being politically correct, fair or polite – just let it rip! Keep writing/speaking until you sense you have emptied out your hurt feelings for the time being.

When you are done writing, take your pages and burn them in your fireplace, outdoor fire pit or even in your sink, if it is deep enough and made of stainless steel. The point is, burn the paper in a safe place. If you have absolutely nowhere you can safely burn your pages, put them through a shredder if you have one, or rip them into tiny unreadable fragments and throw them out. This part of processing your emotions is important. It is a symbolic way of letting the negative feelings go, of releasing and/or transforming them.

After you have finished with this part of the process, let yourself rest... perhaps go for an easy walk in a beautiful outdoor setting or take a bath in Epsom salts and essential oils. In other words, be kind and gentle with yourself. You have just purged toxic emotions from your mind, body and Soul, and you need to take it easy for a little while before you reengage in your usual life activities or move on to the next step in the process.

## F**k It! – Exercise 6
## Breathing Your Emotions – Expansion

This is a more "advanced" exercise, in that it asks you to work on a subtle level. It's not a way to bypass actually expressing your feelings, but it's a way to deal with feelings that come up in an environment where you don't have the privacy or time to scream, cry or write. It's also an exercise to use as a follow up to and a reinforcement of the emotional release work.

By using breath to focus your attention, and visualization, you can release your pain by "watching" your emotions leave your body. Focus on the part of your body that is holding your emotional pain. Breathe in, intentionally directing your breath to the pain. After holding your breath there for a few beats, exhale deeply with the intention of letting the emotion go completely.

Have you watched a tennis match? Some people hit the ball and make audible tones that resonate with the action. You can do the same. Anything that works for you is fine. Experiment with your body, your reactions and your releasing process. As you breathe your pain out, see in your mind's eye the energy of your painful emotion moving out of your body. You may see this energy as a black cloud, jagged shards, or creepy crawlies. Allow the vision to come to you naturally.

As you "see" this energy leaving your body, you will begin to experience relief and a feeling of lightness. You may also find that you feel tired or that the experience brings up tears. Honor yourself in this process. If you need to cry and are in a place where you can do so, got for it. The same goes for resting. Do your best to support yourself as you move through and release your pain.

\*\*\*

## Full-Spectrum Forgiveness

This phase of the process is called "full-spectrum" because it includes everything: forgiving, asking for forgiveness, and releasing your judgments. You will identify and forgive all the judgments you have made against yourself, others, the circumstances, and God/ Higher Power/Spirit/Soul.

Since we are souls living a *human* experience, it is important from the *human* standpoint to forgive others and ask for forgiveness when appropriate. It is the human part of us that takes offense, experiences hurt, and makes judgments. The Soul knows we are all One and that there is no right or wrong, bad or good. It is important to be clear that even if you don't or can't receive an apology from the one who hurt you, you can still move on with your own healing by going through and completing a "full-spectrum" process. You don't have to wait for something that might never happen.

### *Full-Spectrum Forgiveness – Exercise 1*
### *Identifying Your Judgments*

Write down your answers to the following questions:

1. What stories have I told myself about this situation?
2. What assumptions or judgments have I made because of this hurt?

In answer to those two questions, Joseph (example from Chapter One), might have responded, "I don't have power. I lost my power. I am a victim. I get taken advantage of. I'm less of a man."

## Full-Spectrum Forgiveness – Exercise 2
### Being Willing to Let Go

Ask yourself, "Can I let these stories, assumptions and judgments go?"

If your answer is yes, you are ready to move on to Full-Spectrum Forgiveness Exercise 3.

If your answer is no, ask yourself: "Do I want to let my pain and suffering go? What am I willing to do to experience inner freedom?" Go back to the F**k It! phase of this Process, and keep working on transforming your pain through the release exercises. When you have begun to experience some relief from your immediate pain, you will be willing to do the work to complete the 3Fs Process.

## Full-Spectrum Forgiveness – Exercise 3
### Identifying the Real Wound

The next question I have for you may be harder to answer. The question is: "What is the *real* wound?" We all carry emotional wounds, and being able to pinpoint the *real* wound will be instrumental in helping you release the pain and suffering associated with it.

In an effort to get Joseph to lighten up, his wife would poke gentle fun at her often serious husband. He was privately offended by his wife's innocuous teasing and would hold his feelings in while sulking or retreating to another room. He felt she was shaming him.

51

It wasn't until he discovered the real wound underlying his over-sensitivity that he was able to lighten up and see things as they actually were. He believed that what had happened to him as a child was shameful and that if anyone knew about it, they would ridicule him. The more he tried to cover up the truth of the real wound, the more he was triggered by his wife's harmless joking.

He had to learn to detach himself from the upset that was being triggered by his wife's teasing and ask himself, "What does this mean to me? What am I reading into her teasing that causes me to feel so upset and ashamed? What part of me is being triggered/hurt/annoyed by her joking?"

Joseph's false beliefs about himself based on his experience of having been raped as a child had been a part of his identity for so long that they had become a kind of "protection." Once he was able to open up and share with his wife what had happened to him, he was able to let go of his defensive posture and "lighten up." Becoming aware of the *real* wound helped Joseph through the process of accepting, releasing and transforming *that* wound into a scar.

Once your wounds and the assumptions you made about yourself as a result of the trauma you experienced are identified, you will have a better understanding of the false beliefs that have been ruling your life. You can ask yourself the same questions Joseph asked himself in order to identify the real wound:

1. What is this really triggering inside of me?
2. Have I experienced this before?
3. What am I protecting by not letting it go?
4. How would I feel without the wound?
5. How can I transform the wound into a healed scar?

### Full-Spectrum Forgiveness – Exercise 4
### Learning to Forgive Yourself

The core of the 3Fs process is **self-forgiveness.**

Take a deep breath, center your attention in your heart by placing one or both of your hands over your heart-center, and say out loud:

"I forgive myself for judging myself as (assumptions, judgments, stories, limiting beliefs)."

Based on the example of Joseph's assumptions about himself as a result of his traumatic rape, his self-forgiveness might look like:

–  "I forgive myself for judging myself as powerless."
–  "I forgive myself for judging myself as less of a man."
–  "I forgive myself for judging God, believing He had abandoned me."
–  "I forgive myself for judging the perpetrators as cruel."

Of course, this last statement is one of the most difficult ones. It's important to remember that you are not forgiving acts. You are forgiving *your own judgments.*

Continue with your self-forgiveness, repeating the statements that come forward for you until you believe that all of your assumptions, stories, limiting beliefs and judgments have been addressed. You may have to do this many times over many days, weeks, months… until you feel clear. This may involve repeating the same statements or thinking of new ones as you continue with the process.

### Full-Spectrum Forgiveness – Exercise 5
### Reframing Your Judgments

As you go through the self-forgiveness exercise, especially as you get to a place where you are starting to feel genuine forgiveness in your heart, you will want to begin to "reframe" the judgments, assumptions and limiting beliefs you are addressing. When you "reframe" a false or limiting judgment, you are in effect acknowledging a higher truth.

You are taking a higher perspective and choosing the see the essence of the person or the situation rather than the mean or cruel way in which they have treated you. You are choosing to see through the eyes of God; you are accessing your Divine nature. With compassion and empathy, you are choosing to see yourself and the person who hurt you as Divine Beings who are simply having human experiences.

For example, Joseph, after having practiced self-forgiveness by repeating: "I forgive myself for judging myself as less of a man," might have chosen to reframe that particular judgment by saying: "The truth is that I am a whole man, and a deeply sensitive man, who has learned to live from his heart and chooses to share his loving nature with the world."

As with the self-forgiveness exercise, you will ideally want to repeat your reframe out loud. The reframed sentences can be created in response to the judgments that have come forward for clearing, or they can be spontaneous utterances from your Soul. You might find yourself saying something like, "The truth I'm choosing to believe now is that I am/he is/they are Divine beings living a human experience, and we are all doing the best we can according to the level of consciousness we have access to."

This is a profoundly healing aspect of this practice and one that will transform your energy in ways that will astound you! You are a Divine Being, and when you acknowledge this truth and speak from that space inside yourself, you open your heart to the Light and Beauty of Grace.

## Full-Spectrum Forgiveness – Exercise 6
## The Power of the Mirror

I was inspired by Robert Holden and Louise Hay, who both use mirror work for self-acceptance, to use this exercise with my clients. It is particularly powerful if you are having a lot of resistance come up around forgiving.

Stand in front of a mirror, and tell yourself why you feel you can't or won't forgive yourself and the others involved. This will help you see the wound that prevents you from forgiving. Release the wound by looking in the mirror, into your eyes, and practicing the self-forgiveness work. This is an opportunity to love yourself by seeing your essence.

## Full-Forgiveness Spectrum – Exercise 7
## Saying You're Sorry

It is empowering to ask for and receive forgiveness. After doing all of the exercises in the 3Fs Process, if there is someone in your life you feel you have hurt or wronged, let them know how you feel, and ask for their forgiveness. If you cannot get in touch with that person for any reason (if they are dead or you don't know how to contact them), go to your inner sanctuary and communicate with that person either out loud or in writing. Your process will not be hampered if they don't forgive you or if you cannot communicate with them directly. Remember, forgiveness is ultimately for your benefit.

***

# Freedom

This is the Phase in which you get to celebrate yourself and the courage it took for you to re-experience your pain, face it, work through it and transform it through honest self-forgiveness! You are integrating all the disowned aspects of yourself. What was previously a disconnected, destructive and disabled part of your psyche is now transformed. You are experiencing yourself as a whole person, able to love and accept who you are, as well as who you were.

Through forgiveness, you are on your way to awakening. This process is very powerful and can turn a breakdown into a breakthrough, but don't get discouraged if you don't feel immediate relief. Remember that you have the tools to transform any pain, and you have the courage to use them! Congratulations!!

## Freedom – Exercise 1
### Self-Nurturing

Celebrate yourself by taking care of yourself. This may mean getting a pedicure or going for a bike ride, but it can also be as simple as soaking in a bubble bath or taking a nap when you feel tired. The essence of self-nurturing is self-love. How can you show yourself how much you love yourself? If you were your own child, how would you treat yourself? With patience, gentleness and loving kindness!

## Freedom – Exercise 2
### Experiencing Gratitude

Gratitude as a practice is powerful and simple. It is the way to acknowledge all the blessings in your life by taking time each day, or as often as possible, to express your gratitude. You can express gratitude for everything and anything – yourself, your health, your spouse, your child, your animal companion, your best friend, your family, your home, the beautiful day, the delicious meal and on and on…

As with forgiveness, gratitude allows you to immediately access your Divine nature. As you recount all the things and people in your life you are grateful for, your heart opens and your joy expands. If you're able to feel grateful for the growth you've experienced as a result of challenges and life circumstances, the practice of gratitude can completely change your perspective.

## Freedom – Exercise 3
## Expressing Positive Affirmations

Positive affirmations will support your progress and keep your energy uplifted as you open more fully to experiencing inner freedom. Affirmations are most effective when they are written down and stated in the positive, kept simple and concluded with an exclamation point! As with your intentions, I encourage you to post your affirmations around your house, anywhere you will see them frequently. That way you are constantly infused with the positive loving energy they represent!

I recommend beginning your affirmation with "I am..." as in:

- "I am experiencing complete relief from heartache and sadness, as my heart opens to the unending flow of God's Love!"

- "I am experiencing waves of gratitude and joy washing over my entire being as I surrender to the Grace of God!"

- "I am opening my heart, mind and Soul to the Love I am!"

- "I am accepting myself and others as they are!"

- "I am experiencing forgiveness in all shapes and forms!"

- "I am setting myself free!"

## Freedom – Exercise 4
### Creating Your Forgiveness Vision Board

This a way to expand on and update the "Ideal Scene" you mentally created before you started this process. A Vision Board is a collage of images you have collected (magazine pictures, photographs, printed Internet images) or created (photographed, drawn, painted) that represent something you want.

Your Forgiveness Vision Board will represent how you want to feel after you have completed the 3Fs Process. For example, you may find that images of hearts, scenes from nature, or two people hugging evoke the energy and the feelings you want to experience. Let your creativity go wild! Have fun with this project.

Use a big board as your foundation, and spend some time collecting images and adding them to your board as your vision for yourself and your life of freedom expands. You may want to hang your Vision Board where you can easily see it every day, so it is a constant reminder of what you have been working toward. Or you may choose to put it in your private sanctuary where you can spend time meditating on the beautiful images you have assembled.

## Freedom – Exercise 5
### The Acid Test

This last exercise is the "acid test" and is based on the concepts Joseph Murphy explores in his book *The Power of Your Subconscious Mind*. We test gold with acid to find out whether it is real gold. We can test ourselves to see whether we have attained our own inner gold: forgiveness.

How does it work? Simple… if you experience no more pain when recalling the situation that caused you pain and hurt, you have achieved your own inner gold. If you cannot wish the person who hurt you well, or if the presence or the name of the person causes you pain, you still have more work to do to achieve your inner gold.

## Spinning Pain into Gold

Joseph was always trying to be the champion of justice. He protected people who were hurt, and he was a gentleman in the truest sense of the word. He never took his anger out on others, but the energy he had to expend in order to keep his secret – to battle the monsters that lived inside of him – was quite literally killing him from the inside out.

Until he was ready to face the pain he had experienced as a boy, and consciously detach himself from the labels he adopted at that young age, he couldn't use that energy to heal and transform the pain. He couldn't use it to serve himself or the world. After having worked with Joseph for quite some time, I can say that he is now ready to use his experience to serve others who have gone through similar traumas.

We cannot help others from a "crucifixion" condition. We have to be in "resurrection" consciousness if we want to serve others. We can't help others when we ride through life in the victim seat; we can only help others from an empowered place.

Joseph's forgiveness work is an example of how something painful can give birth to something extraordinary. Forgiveness empowers us to dig deep inside to find greater inner strength and courage. It encourages us to find love in the middle of horror. We can't change the past, but we can act as agents of future change. When the doors of the heart open wide to healing and love, we experience transformation – that path to awakening.

## Detaching From Our Judgments

The following story illustrates the importance of being aware of everything that happens around us, and is an example of how events that happen outside of our own lives can trigger upsets and judgments inside of us. By identifying the judgments and working to release them, we can train ourselves to do the same in our daily lives. This doesn't mean we have to deny the sad things we hear about in the news, but by detaching from our judgments, we are able to reside in a place inside that is more peaceful. As a result, we are better able to take action to help others or touch their lives with love.

The University of California, Santa Barbara has a beautiful, lush campus overlooking the ocean in central California. It isn't far from my home and also very close to my heart. My son Seba graduated from UCSB about nine years ago, and I enjoyed driving up the beautiful Southern California coast to visit him.

Not long ago, the University was all over the news because a student went on a rampage, stabbed his roommates to death and shot everyone he came in contact with. He eventually killed himself. I could not hold back my tears. In just one minute, everything changed. The images were too much for my aching heart. Every victim's face, including the assassin's, made me feel extremely sad. I felt deep compassion for them all. The parents... how would they ever find peace again? What is forgiveness in this kind of situation, and how can it help ease the pain?

The face of the father of one of the victims haunted me for several days. I turned on the radio and there he was, saying that it was important to have gun control laws. The right to have a life was more important than the right to bear arms. I wondered how someone with psychological issues could buy and keep so many guns.

As I watched the news reports, I thought about how these kinds of violent events affect us, and often trigger our own unresolved issues. I tried, without much success, to release my judgments. Believe me, I had to go to the core of my issues, and with conscious intention, let them go! Let me be clear that my desire to release my judgments didn't mean I condoned what had happened.

By releasing my judgments, I knew I would be better able to focus on what could be done to prevent things like that from happening in the future. Focusing on the "whys" wasn't going to help. "Be part of the solution and not the problem," I told myself. While I was absorbed in my thoughts, I overheard Anderson Cooper on the news saying that the father of the 20-year-old man who was shot to death was asking people to offer condolences to the parents of the killer!

Oh, my God! Only four days after the shooting, in the midst of his profound suffering, he was taking a step toward love and healing, not hatred! Hatred would have been so much easier. In the midst of his grief, he chose love. What did that mean? If he'd felt hatred in his heart, he could not have done what he did.

Compassion helps us understand and ease the pain. Revenge does not heal the pain. It may feel like it does momentarily, but it does not heal the open wound, only love does.

## Build Your House on Rock

*"Everyone then who hears these words of mine and does them will be like a wise man who built his house on the rock. And the rain fell, and the floods came, and the winds blew and beat on*

*that house, but it did not fall, because it had been founded on the rock. And everyone who hears these words of mine and does not do them will be like a foolish man who built his house on the sand. And the rain fell, and the floods came, and the winds blew and beat against that house, and it fell, and great was the fall of it."*
—Matthew 7:24-27

Love is the rock, and in order to have that rock to build your house on, you have to use forgiveness. Other people may betray you or act in a hurtful way, but if your heart remains open, you will be capable of enduring the storms that might hit your house.

That means using forgiveness and being in "forgiveness shape" so that your heart can remain open. Trusting and keeping your heart open doesn't mean that you don't take action to protect yourself. You take action by attuning to your inner wisdom, to the God inside of you, to your higher source, and using your common sense and discernment (different from judgment!) to decide on the best action to take.

You follow your internal GPS and consciously decide whether you are going to enter into certain relationships or associate with certain people. You quiet your mind through prayer and meditation, so your intuition is clear. You listen to your internal guidance. When you pray, you ask God for guidance and direction; when you meditate you listen for the answers.

Being "forgiving" does not mean we don't take care of ourselves. Actually that's the first thing we need to do before we can take care of others. Forgiving means that we have the tools to keep our hearts open to the experience of love, acceptance and compassion despite the storms we will inevitably go through in life. Forgiveness serves us by allowing us to release the bitterness that hurt, disappointment and betrayal leave in our heart.

> *"Anger is like flowing water; there's nothing wrong with it as long as you let it flow. Hate is like stagnant water; anger that you denied yourself the freedom to feel, the freedom to flow; water that you gathered in one place and left to forget. Stagnant water becomes dirty, stinky, disease-ridden, poisonous, deadly; that is your hate. On flowing water travels little paper boats; paper boats of forgiveness. Allow yourself to feel anger, allow your waters to flow, along with all the paper boats of forgiveness. Be human."*
> —C. JoyBell C.

❖ ❖ ❖

CHAPTER THREE

# SELF-FORGIVENESS

*"The truth is, unless you let go, unless you forgive yourself,*
*unless you forgive the situation, unless you realize that*
*the situation is over, you cannot move forward."*
—Steve Maraboli – *Life, the Truth, and Being Free*

## My Time as a Prison Volunteer

There are no words to describe the experience I had as a volunteer in a men's prison. These particular men were all long-term prisoners serving 25 years to life, most of them for murder or for being accessories to murder. The majority of them were seeking a way to feel like valuable human beings. They wanted to find a way to feel peaceful and successful, even "in the cage," and they wondered if inner peace was possible for them.

To get into the Level 4 section of the prison where we did our volunteer counseling work, the prisoners had to have renounced their past gang affiliations, distanced themselves from their past behaviors, given up any addictions, and started the process of letting go of their anger and pain. This, of course, is always easier said than done, but they all knew that they couldn't go back to Levels 1, 2, or 3, where they would probably have been killed. The lower levels of the prison are tremendously violent with "inside rules" that the men must follow or be severely punished by gang members.

Some of the common threads shared by the inmates included extremely poor parenting, emotional and/or physical violence in their homes and severe socioeconomic disadvantages. These men had grown up as the "walking wounded" – poor children with few opportunities. In addition, many of them were illegal immigrants, or their families were illegal, which meant that they never had visitors.

Some had been severely abused – physically, emotionally and mentally. Almost all of them reported having turned, at one point or another, to drinking, drugs or gangs. After many decades of living in constant fear of death at any moment – both outside and inside of prison – these men in Level 4 had consciously made the decision to follow a more peaceful path. This led them to participate in the programs offered by the prison, which included non-violent communication workshops, religious services and 12-step programs that asked them to make amends to the people, or families of the people, they had victimized.

The other common thread that connected the men is that almost all of them were looking for a second chance in life. "Aren't we all?" I said to myself as I walked through the wire fence on that cold November afternoon.

Our pilot program in the men's prison consisted of 76 inmates and a total of 40 volunteers. There were no funds for the program, so the volunteers covered the costs (and have continued to do so for the last ten years since the initial program launched). Each of us felt called to do the work for different reasons. In my case, I wished to open the hearts of the participants and bring some light into the darkness.

There is a ripple effect that occurs when you help another person. By touching one person's life, you have the opportunity to touch many lives, even if you never know who they are. Some of the prisoners I worked with told me that they had taught the transformational tools we brought to them to other prisoners who missed our workshops.

Some of the prisoners became so excited by the work we did with them that they shared the tools we taught with their own families outside "the cage." It was like lighting one candle that was then passed around and used to light other candles with the flame of hope, love and transformation.

The feedback we received from many of the prisoners was that our three-day workshop was practical, useful and impactful. Some commented that it was better than anything they had learned in the eight years they had been taking self-help programs at the prison. I sat in awe, with tear-filled eyes, as I listened to several of them share during the workshop. The sounds of their voices and the stories they shared will stay with me forever.

## Johnny's Story

As I sat in the middle of the huge gym surrounded by the 76 men, I could see that they all wanted a way out. This is where I first met Johnny. He had already been in prison for a long time. He had done a lot of work on himself and had been able to create a decent life in the prison by reading and participating in as many self-help programs as he could.

He worked inside the prison in order to have a sense of purpose, and had already done a considerable amount of forgiveness work. Still, he craved inner peace. He was haunted by the image of his fiancée's face as he pointed a gun at her and pulled the trigger. He'd murdered her 25 years earlier in a moment of uncontrolled rage, but the image still repeated itself in his frequent nightmares.

The first time I spoke with him, I was struck by the wisdom of his words. He had obviously contemplated his actions a great deal. He was very cautious and distrustful at first, so I tried not to push him. He had to "measure" me and make sure he felt safe.

Johnny spoke perfect English, but suddenly, he switched to Spanish, speaking to me in my native tongue, as he made a declaration I will never forget: "nunca voy a ser libre" (I will never be free). At that very moment, the bell rang for us to break for lunch. Without saying anything, we got our food and sat next to each other in a corner outside the gym. He looked at me, tears rolling down his cheeks, and with immeasurable sorrow, shared the details of his painful experience.

He was abused as a child over and over again, and just like my client, Joseph, he'd kept it a secret. In Johnny's case, though, keeping the secret eventually caused him to turn to violence. As a young man, he had been quick to react in anger, and he never felt he was "man enough." So he'd continually tried to prove himself by acting "macho."

On the night he murdered his fiancée, she'd come home late, and he accused her of cheating on him. In the middle of their argument, he grabbed a gun and shot her without thinking.

"Johnny, have you worked on self-forgiveness?" I asked as tenderly as I could.

"Yes, a lot," he said, as his voice cracked through his tears. "Clara, I can't understand why you look at me like I'm a normal person. Why don't I see hate and fear in your eyes like I do with everybody else?"

"I see your essence, Johnny, not your actions." He looked at me puzzled. I asked, "What happened when you worked on self-forgiveness?"

"I have asked forgiveness of my fiancée's family, and I know it would be good to forgive myself, but Clara…" He looked into my eyes. "I'm a monster. Would you forgive a monster?"

I knew we were pressed for time, so I needed to speak fast. "Johnny, you are not a monster. You're paying your debt to society, and I understand that if you could go back in time, you would change your actions."

"You don't get it. What's done is done! I took a life!"

"Yes, I know that, but I also know that tormenting yourself won't bring her back. You can't change the past, but you can use the past as a force for transformation. Then, you can use that energy to help others here. If you continue to believe you're a monster, you'll never be able to help anyone else."

"A lot of men in prison have been abused," he told me. "They feel like their manhood was stolen from them. It's hard enough to deal with that in the outside world. Dealing with that in the cage is a whole other story. You have to prove you're a man at all times, and that leads to an awful lot of violence."

He continued to tell me about his experiences and how he had been able to accept his journey, and even forgive his abuser. "But what I did … that tortures me every day. It's worse than being locked up physically. I want to forgive myself, but I know I don't deserve it."

"We all deserve it, Johnny. All of us. So can you do it, Johnny? Can you forgive yourself?"

"I need her permission, and she's f\*\*king dead! God won't let me forgive myself." He hid his head in his hands.

I wanted to hold his hand, but of course, we weren't allowed to do that. Nonetheless, I put a hand on his shoulder, praying the guards wouldn't see. I asked God to guide me and said, "Johnny, close your eyes, and ask God to guide you to wherever your fiancée is in spirit. Tell her whatever you want to say to her. You can do it, Johnny. God is inside you."

He broke into tears as he spoke to his fiancée. He asked her for forgiveness, barely able to get the words out because his pain was so immense.

We had just a few minutes left, so I said, "Johnny, wherever she is, she can hear you. You don't have to tie yourself to a physical answer from her in order to set yourself free. Killing yourself inside will not do anyone any good. Give yourself permission to forgive yourself. You're the one who has to grant that permission. You hold the key. Use it, you deserve it." Then the bell rang, and we had to quickly return to the gym.

I wanted to continue my work with Johnny, but I couldn't break the rules. I had to wait for instructions from the authorities. *If it's meant to be, it will be,* I thought to myself.

As we began the after lunch session, I saw Johnny on the other side of the room working with another inmate and one of my fellow volunteers. He looked like he was speaking from an open and vulnerable place. *That's a good thing,* I thought.

When the last part of the workshop on Sunday afternoon arrived, it was time to work on the most challenging aspect of our work – compassionate self-forgiveness. As luck would have it, I found myself seated in front of Johnny again. This time, he looked calm, and his eyes held a different expression than they had two days earlier.

Once again, he asked me, "Clara, can I let the monster go? Can I really forgive myself?"

"Are you willing to do that, Johnny?" I countered.

"Yes," he replied softly. "It's about time. It's not about carrying the cross anymore. It's about allowing myself to experience resurrection."

"Beautiful words... forgiveness is resurrection, another chance at life."

He read the instructions on our worksheet and looked at me again. He sighed painfully, "No, I can't forgive what I did..."

"Johnny, just follow the instructions on the worksheet, and you will start to feel the power of forgiveness – maybe not today or next week, but eventually. And when you feel it, the doors inside you will open wide, and even in this place, you will experience a sense of freedom. Remember that this isn't about forgiving your actions in the past. You are forgiving the judgments you have about every single thing, including yourself."

The room was filled with people practicing compassionate self-forgiveness, and everyone was immersed in their own experience. I could hear soft cries echoing through the room as people left huge boulders of pain and guilt behind.

Johnny started to identify his judgments one by one. "I'm a monster. I don't deserve to live. I'm a killer."

I guided him to place his hand over his heart and say, "I forgive myself for judging myself as a monster. I forgive myself for judging myself as unworthy of life."

Johnny broke down again and said, "I'm a killer. I'm a killer."

"I know this is difficult, Johnny. You have killed. I know that. But you are more than that. You are not your actions. You are not your behaviors. Yes, you're fully responsible for your actions and behaviors, and that's the reason you've spent so many years in this place. But you can transcend what you did in the past. You don't have to define yourself as a killer for the rest of your life. You are your essence, and your essence or Soul is still whole. Detach yourself from the masks you wear, and cut the strings that keep the masks attached to your face. Forgiveness acts like the scissors that cut the strings."

He took a deep breath and said with more conviction, "I forgive myself for judging myself as a killer, for thinking that is who I really am." He repeated it several times, and the strings that held the masks began to loosen and fall away. His true essence timidly began to emerge from hiding.

The time we had together ended quickly, and since we had to follow strict protocols, there was no real time to say goodbye. Johnny wrote his name on a small piece of paper, handed it to me, and said, "Please let me know how I can continue with this work."

I sent him books about trauma, child abuse, and forgiveness. I didn't hear back from him for a long time, but eventually I received a letter. He wrote that he had been doing the forgiveness work day and night, unearthing his judgments and letting go of his need to rationalize them.

He wrote that he would repeat over and over to himself, "I have killed, but that's not who I am." He also disclosed that when he was in the prison showers, he often re-experienced the memories of his abuse, so he would say to himself, "I was abused, but I'm not a victim. I forgive myself for judging myself as a victim."

I had explained to Johnny that when we are victimized, we identify ourselves as victims, which keeps us stuck in that persona. In order to empower ourselves and let go of being a victim, we must feel our feelings, remove all judgments, and forgive ourselves.

He went on in his letter to explain that as he lay down to sleep at night, he would say to himself, "I forgive myself for judging my abusers as monsters. I forgive myself for judging myself as a monster." The old feelings were still sometimes present, but as he believed the thoughts and judgments accompanying the feelings less and less, he began to experience some relief, an inkling of inner freedom. He shared that he repeated to himself a bit of advice I'd given him: "Don't believe everything you think."

He wrote that he'd read all of the books I sent and was very grateful for the work we had done together. He was feeling better than ever and had joined several support groups, hopeful that he'd be able to assist others who were feeling lost, confused and depressed.

"Life is not easy here," he confessed, "but I want to make something out of it. I go to sleep, and I feel at peace most of the time. I go to the showers, and I feel like a whole man again – not less, not more. My painful stories of abuse don't define me anymore. You have brought me hope."

## Guilt and Shame

What happens if, like Johnny, you are the offender? We have all been the "offender" at different points in our lives, haven't we? We have all hurt someone else to some degree, either on purpose or inadvertently.

Yes, you can ask for forgiveness from the person you hurt. You can say, "I'm sorry." You can show that you're eager to repair the mistake and do better next time. You can insist that you're willing to change. While this may be an important part of your process, you cannot count on the other person to forgive you. Whether or not they do so is part of their own process; it isn't part of yours. You can't demand forgiveness from someone you have hurt, and you can't hold yourself hostage based on someone else's decision. This is why self-forgiveness is so important.

Without self-forgiveness, guilt and shame will keep you chained to pain and suffering. Without self-forgiveness, the best you can do is cover the shame you feel with even more shame. When you live with shame, you cannot focus your love and energy on rebirth. From a psychological point of view, guilt is an emotion. It's an internal state of mind and certainly not a good motivator. Neither is shame, which comes out of guilt. According to psychologist, Erik Erikson, guilt emerges in life between the ages of three and five. Depending on the experience each of us has at that early age, guilt is imprinted inside of us in a certain way.

Does guilt have any value at all? Well, there is "healthy" guilt, and "unhealthy" guilt. With healthy guilt, we acknowledge what we did and take responsibility for it, looking ahead to the future in order to avoid making the same mistake again.

With unhealthy guilt, we beat ourselves up for what we did. Let's look at a simple example: You might feel guilty for having eaten too much cake, and as you chastise yourself for it, you find yourself wanting more cake in order to self-soothe from your own negativity. The many millions of people who struggle with dieting know that vicious circle all too well!

Unhealthy guilt keeps us stuck so that we can't evolve. Sometimes people even feel guilty for feeling happy when there are others who are unhappy. Have you ever felt something like that? It's human, but it isn't helpful, especially if the guilt prevents you from moving forward in your life. Many of us first experienced these destructive patterns in childhood. Only with awareness of the patterns can we release the guilt and be free.

In Johnny's case, I knew that he could turn his overpowering guilt into a sense of personal responsibility. This means that he could transform the unhealthy guilt into healthy guilt that would no longer keep him stuck in self-judgment but allow him to do something productive with his life.

Usually, when we have done something to harm someone else, we either justify our behavior and make excuses or become stuck in a self-flagellating (unhealthy) guilt. We then become victims of our own guilt. The lesson Johnny had to learn was a very painful one. Nevertheless, learning it was an opportunity to finally end the cycle of pain and anger he had endured for the majority of his life.

What about when guilt leads to shame? Shame is also an emotion that keeps us paralyzed and stuck. It's a much deeper emotion than embarrassment. It comes from an old word meaning "to cover." It is the pain of having done or experienced something dishonorable or improper, and we often experience it even when we are the ones who have been victimized.

My client, Joseph, who was raped as a child and then repressed his feelings. He experienced physical and psychological pain, as well as guilt and shame. He internalized the experience as something that diminished him as a man. He decided that if nobody knew about it, he would be safe. He "covered up" what he "judged" internally as shameful. The hidden shame became part of his identity, and at times dictated his actions and reactions. Shame is one of the most difficult emotions to release because we feel ashamed about feeling shame. Joseph didn't have anything to be ashamed of, but he believed something different. So that was his reality.

When we feel shame, we disown parts of ourselves. Psychiatrist Carl Jung called these disowned parts "shadow selves." These shadow aspects of ourselves can take over our personalities and cause us to "act out" or behave in ways we don't really want to behave. When we become aware of these parts and forgive ourselves, we are able to integrate our shadow selves so that they no longer compel us to "act out."

*"Self-love has very little to do with how you feel about your outer self. It's about accepting all of yourself."*
—Tyra Banks

## Accepting Our Humanness

According to Archbishop Desmond Tutu, in the Xhosa language, asking for forgiveness translates to "I ask for peace." That's what forgiveness gives us – peace. We cannot create peace in the world until we create peace in our own lives. Inner peace starts with self-forgiveness. As Gandhi put it, you have to, "Be the change that you wish to see in the world." When we no longer identify ourselves with the misfortunes, traumas and wounds of the past, we create peace from the inside out. A forgiving world starts from within.

Most of us walk around in a state of inner turmoil. And most of us tend to define ourselves by our flaws, which is why it is so much easier to remember criticisms than compliments. Even defining ourselves by our successes is like standing on a very fragile precipice. One mistake, and we fall to failure.

Success can be a source of inspiration, but not a reliable definition of who we are. We are human *beings*, not human *doings*.

Unconditional self-love is not based on what we do. The truth is that most of us don't feel safe unless we're perfect. Our imperfections cause us pain, especially when we believe others are judging us. We see ourselves as imperfect and therefore unlovable or unacceptable when we make mistakes.

Since we spend a lot more time focusing on our flaws, self-forgiveness is complicated. When we fixate on our imperfections, we feel unworthy, sometimes not worthy of our own forgiveness, and sometimes not even worthy of love. Most of the time, the underlying belief is that we cannot be forgiven unless we're perfect. Until we feel we are deserving, we find it hard to give ourselves permission to forgive ourselves.

Many people also believe that the only way to be responsible for something they have done wrong is to perpetuate their feelings of guilt forever. What they fail to understand is that guilt and responsibility are two different things. Taking full responsibility is important because it empowers us, but holding on to guilt only keeps us locked in the past. The combination of self-forgiveness and responsibility frees us, opening the doors to new possibilities to move on and become more spiritually evolved.

There is a phrase in the Bible (Mark 3:25) that says, "And if a house be divided against itself, that house cannot stand." The same holds true for human beings. When we turn against ourselves, we live with inner turmoil. If you're stuck in self-blame, guilt or self-hatred, you are losing power every day as your energy is expended against yourself.

How can we love others when we don't love ourselves? How can we give what we don't have? How can we experience wholeness if we are split apart inside? Self-forgiveness is what melts the walls that separate us from love.

You probably know someone who feels bitterness toward their own soul – or perhaps you experience this yourself. Holding resentment against yourself for past mistakes leads to self-loathing, and that further inhibits your capacity for happiness and freedom, as well as emotional and physical health.

Acceptance is the first step toward forgiving ourselves – acceptance of our own humanness. When we are able to accept what we have done and what we have experienced, we can take productive action toward changing the future. We can then make decisions from a place of compassion, clarity and inner peace.

## Tracy's Story

Tracy, an outgoing middle-aged woman and a friend of mine, came to me desperate for help. She had been married for a long time, and the marriage had been pretty stable. But her husband had recently become distant. She thought he was going through a midlife crisis, so she tried to help. But the more she attempted to get him to open up, the more distant he became.

Then, at his birthday party, she noticed that he kept leaving the party to talk or text on his phone. She had never had reason to doubt his fidelity before, but her suspicions were aroused, so she grabbed the phone out of his hand and sure enough, she saw a text message from another woman. The emotional pain was lacerating. He tried to deny it, but the evidence spoke for itself.

Needless to say, they had a big fight, but the argument ended when he made a firm declaration that he wanted to stay with Tracy. He told her he still loved her very much, but that he felt lost and confused. He insisted the other woman meant nothing to him and asked for his wife's forgiveness.

Suddenly, Tracy's husband, who had so recently been distant and uncommunicative, was present, talking and eager to make the marriage work. They came to see me to work on converting expectations into agreements and agreements into commitments. I worked with them to help them rebuild a conscious relationship where both of them felt loved, respected and heard. One of their commitments to each other was to cultivate a relationship based on honesty and integrity from that moment forward.

After that session, Tracy and her husband each did the forgiveness work on their own, and things looked promising … until I got a tearful call from Tracy. She asked if she could see me right away. She arrived sobbing. "It's been so hard for me to move on from this. I really felt like I had forgiven him, but out of the blue, I started feeling so upset. When I tried to talk to him about it, he just got mad. He seemed so insensitive to my pain, and we argued."

Tracy and I began a process called "healing memories" to try to discover what had triggered her upset. She closed her eyes and remembered that while driving home earlier in the evening she'd seen a billboard with a text message emblazoned on it. Seeing any text message at all triggered her to remember the text message from the other woman on her husband's phone.

"I hate phones! Why do people need to text all the time?" she cried.

Then she disclosed that right before she called me, her husband had been on the phone for a long time talking to his business partner. It reminded her again of the text from the other woman. In spite of all the progress she and her husband had made in their marriage, Tracy's current emotional pain came from the fact that she still didn't trust her husband.

We continued the exercise, bringing up more memories. Tracy saw herself as a young woman who did a lot for her family but did not feel appreciated for it. She shared that she could never satisfy her father no matter how hard she tried.

She started to cry and exclaimed, "Everything is so unfair!"

Tracy recalled that her father used to blame her for things she hadn't done. This memory evoked the words, "I'm not enough. I'm not enough no matter how much I do. No matter how much I love them, it's never enough. I wasn't enough for him." In that moment, we found the connection between what she'd experienced with her father and what she was experiencing with her husband.

The deep pain that her husband's infidelity had triggered was a belief that she wasn't enough. In order to heal this, we began a process during which Tracy expressed compassion and love for her younger self. Only then was she ready to work on self-forgiveness. It wasn't about her husband anymore; it was about herself, about the little girl inside who never felt that her father appreciated her. At first, Tracy had trouble seeing the truth of that.

"Forgive myself? He's the one who had the affair! He doesn't deserve my forgiveness! It's not fair…" she said while sobbing inconsolably.

"Yes, Tracy, I know, and you said you have already forgiven him." Using her words, I said, "Was that enough?"

She screamed in response: "No, it wasn't f**king enough! Nothing I do is f**king enough! And it is not enough that he keeps saying 'I'm sorry.' I want him to feel my pain… only then will I be able to be at peace! He doesn't get how much pain I feel inside."

"Tracy, I understand your pain and sorrow, but is it true that he needs to feel your pain to be at peace?"

"I don't know…" she muttered. "Maybe not… So why isn't it enough that he's sorry? Why can't I release the pain and wash it away with his apologies?"

"Because he's feeling his own pain, and what he feels won't release your own judgments and pain. That's the reason his apologies are not enough."

With her hand over her heart and my hand over her hand, Tracy began to repeat: "I forgive myself for judging myself as unfair. I forgive myself for judging my father, my family and my husband as unfair." She cried some more. "I forgive myself for judging life as unfair. I forgive myself for judging God as unfair. I forgive myself for judging what I do as not enough. I forgive myself for believing that nothing I do is ever enough for me or for others."

Then, with a deep sigh, she finally said, "I forgive myself for judging my husband as not doing enough for our marriage. I forgive myself for judging myself as not enough of a daughter, sister, spouse, mother, woman."

Then, I guided her to the affirmation that would set her free: "I'm enough. I am a soul having a human experience, and I'm doing the best that I can just like everybody else."

Tracy came back a few weeks later and shared with me that the situation was improving. She continued to work on releasing her judgments and freeing herself from the burden of feeling that she was not enough. Eventually, she was able to see the situation from a different perspective, and she no longer related to her husband from a position of not being enough. She had also stopped judging her husband as not enough. She realized that they were both enough.

For Tracy's husband, self-forgiveness was an especially difficult process. He had caused his wife's emotional suffering, and he had to acknowledge that she was trying very hard to trust him again. But her efforts only made his guilt worsen.

"Would it be easier for you to forgive yourself if Tracy hadn't found out about your affair?" I asked him.

"Yes," he said. For him, facing Tracy's judgment of him made his own judgment of himself even stronger.

It took some time for him to release all of his judgments against himself, Tracy, the other woman and the situation. Once he'd gone through that process, the guilt began to ease, which provided a fresh start for the marriage.

In an effort to release all judgments, Tracy put a Rumi quote on their refrigerator that read, "Beyond the right doing and the wrong doing, there is a field; I will meet you there."

She invited her husband to meet her in that "field" where she could see that what he'd done was not intended to hurt her. It was actually about him, not her. They also acknowledged that sometimes they had to agree to disagree and that disagreement didn't have to define who they were as a couple or create distance. Open and honest conversations were the key to meeting in "Rumi's field." They were able to meet there to talk about their problems rationally so that they could make clear and loving decisions about what they wanted for the next phase of their lives together.

Each of them continued to work on self-forgiveness for all of the judgments they had placed on themselves and others. In order to do so, they didn't have to like what had happened in their marriage, but they had to learn to accept it. They each then had the power inside of themselves to make clear choices about the marriage and everything else in their lives.

The choices we make when we are in "Rumi's field" are not conditioned by our old wiring. True forgiveness and self-forgiveness are choices that are not attached to any condition. That's where freedom lies. I know this because I experienced it in my own marriage.

From a spiritual psychology perspective, all forgiveness is self-forgiveness. If we did not judge another person or an incident as "bad" or "wrong," forgiveness wouldn't be necessary, would it? Even when we say, "I forgive you," there is a judgment attached to it because no forgiveness would be necessary without the judgment that came before.

Full-Spectrum Forgiveness goes beyond simple forgiveness to the release of judgments so that there is no feeling of superiority or inferiority. There is only love and freedom. Full-Spectrum Forgiveness gives us a clean slate in life, which helps us thrive in our lives.

## My Own Story

When I learned of my husband's affair and the son it produced, I was in shock. This was yet another challenge in a list of challenges our family was facing at the time. We were dealing with health issues, financial difficulties, my parents' move, and on and on. I had the tools to work through the forgiveness process, but would I use them?

I spent a couple of days crying, grieving the life I had lost. I tried to rationalize by telling myself we all make mistakes. But, a son?! I couldn't hold on to my rationalizations. A son was just too much to bear. Was this some sort of a punishment? Our seemingly "perfect" family wasn't so perfect after all.

I went at dawn to Laguna Beach to touch the beautiful and soothing waters there. It rained that day – yes, in Southern California.

The tears came up from my heart and out of my eyes as the rain poured over my head. I realized that I blamed and judged myself for so many things. I didn't love myself the way I loved others. I was a prisoner in my own homemade cage – not a cage like Johnny's, but certainly a cage of a sort. I wanted to cut the chains that kept me locked inside my own self-blame.

I began bathing my heart with compassion for the hurts I had experienced, the fears, the shame for not being perfect, for not always doing the right thing. The unconditional love started to grow as the blame and shame faded away. The lightness of my heart expanded. It was a strange and wonderful feeling.

I sat in silence for hours while I cried. Then, I finally started to use the most powerful tool for healing I know – self-forgiveness. I repeated, "I forgive myself for judging my husband for his hiding. I forgive myself for judging him as imperfect. I forgive myself for judging my life as not perfect. I forgive myself for judging life as unfair. I forgive myself for hiding. I forgive myself for judging myself as not perfect. I forgive myself for believing I had to be perfect. I forgive myself for believing my husband had to be perfect. I forgive myself for believing our lives had to be perfect. I forgive myself for judging myself for judging my life as not perfect the way it is."

The sun began to rise, as the light was rising inside me. Releasing all judgments is an extraordinarily freeing feeling. There is no need to see anything as better or worse than anything else. It just is.

Even to this day, I get goosebumps when I think of my experience in Laguna Beach. I feel such gratitude for it. I discovered that I could overcome terrible pain and let go of all judgments. I would like to tell you that it was easy for me to release my judgments, but I'd be lying. The process itself was simple, but it took daily practice until the release was complete. That day on the beach was a powerful beginning. I learned that forgiving ourselves takes commitment. I learned that the path to peace and freedom is in letting go and fully accepting ourselves, others and our life circumstances as they are. And it's so, so worth it!

## You Are Forgiveness

As you can see, these different scenarios all have the same ending. Johnny had to let go of his misidentification with the "monster" persona, Tracy had to detach herself from the "I'm not enough" mentality, Joseph had to let go of the idea that he was not safe if anybody found out what happened to him as a child, and I had to release the idea that I had to be perfect to deserve love.

In order to detach ourselves from the false images we create in our minds, we must feel our feelings, stay with the pain, honor the hurt, and compassionately let the judgments go. Yes, all of them! That is what self-forgiveness is all about. Forgiveness is great. Self-forgiveness is a "survival of the soul" skill, and Full-Spectrum Forgiveness opens the doors to awakening. It is the "pill" you take to heal "the pain code" that was imprinted on your heart and unconscious mind when the hurt or trauma occurred. When you let go and allow yourself to move into the peace of self-forgiveness and embrace it fully, you ARE forgiveness.

## Self-Forgiveness Exercise

While delving into the liberating process of self-forgiveness, remember that your suffering resides in the judgments themselves, so it is up to you to dissolve and release them. Even though we explored this process in Chapter Two, I encourage you to revisit this exercise. Self-forgiveness is a powerful tool that takes time and dedication to master.

It is very important to send the right message to the brain. Complete this exercise by filling in the blanks with what you feel you need to forgive. Use the examples in this chapter to guide you.

I judge myself as _____.

I judge my behavior as _____.

I want to forgive myself for _____.

(Notice the difference you feel when you say, "I want to…" as opposed to, "I have to…" The willingness you experience when you want to forgive allows you to benefit fully from the healing process.)

Once you have identified your judgments, start the self-forgiveness process. Remember that this is a tool, and you will need to practice it regularly in order to develop this skill. Even if you don't feel anything at first, don't feel discouraged. You will eventually begin to feel lighter, happier and less judgmental. You might even find that you forget the cause of your emotional pain.

Give yourself the proper time and space for this work. When an emotion rises to the surface, identify where the feeling seems to reside in your body. Then, focus your breath on that area. Emotions become stuck in our bodies, and self-forgiveness aids in releasing that stuck energy.

Forgive whatever feelings emerge as you participate in this process. Don't brush the emotions away. Welcome them, feel them and accept them. Only through self-forgiveness will the feelings move on.

I forgive myself for judging my behavior as _____.

I forgive myself for judging myself as _____.

I forgive myself for judging _____ as _____.

Is there anything else you'd like to say to yourself to facilitate your self-forgiveness?

_____

_____

_____

_____

_____

_____

_____

_____

_____

_____

_____

_____

*"And the day came when the risk to remain tight in a bud was more painful than the risk it took to blossom."*
—Anais Nin

✦ ✦ ✦

# CHAPTER FOUR

# WHY YOU SHOULD FORGIVE THE UNFORGIVABLE

*"Forgiveness is a radical act, but it is certainly not weakness.*
*By forgiving, we do not grant victory to those who wronged us; instead,*
*we surrender the aspect of mind that is blocking divine connection.*
*Not forgiving, then, is granting victory to those who wronged us,*
*in that we allow them to shape our reality."*
—Marianne Williamson – *The Law of Divine Compensation*

S ome actions seem to be simply unforgivable … or are they? How do we forgive Hitler, for example? The "should" in the title of this chapter has nothing to do with morality or obligation. It speaks to the idea that there are real inner benefits to be experienced in releasing judgments of others through deep forgiveness, even those who have committed unforgivable acts.

***

I have asked hundreds of people, including family, friends, colleagues, clients, people who call in during my radio show, and even strangers: "What is it that you personally cannot forgive? What acts do you consider unforgivable?"

The responses to the first question have varied according to the experiences and "lenses" through which each individual viewed life. The majority of answers ranged from betrayal and infidelity to abandonment and abuse. The answers to the second question encompassed acts that are generally considered to be extremely cruel and abhorrent. These acts are often considered "crimes against humanity," and included rape, torture, slavery and genocide.

Some of the reasons I heard for WHY certain people/actions could never be forgiven were:

1. If I forgive, then I am condoning the act and letting the person who committed it off the hook. Furthermore, it isn't fair that the perpetrator be excused for what he/she did. In other words: I am a doormat and my forgiveness will put me in the position to be abused again.

2. I have to hold on to my anger to assure that I won't make the same mistake. In other words: My anger is my protection.

3. My anger assures me that the person who hurt me will never be in my life again. If I forgive the person who hurt me, he/she will hurt me again. In other words: My anger is my protection.

4. This is the truth of what happened to me and it is my story. In other words: I Identify with the story… who would I be without my pain and suffering?

## Understanding Is the First Step to Acceptance

In the beginning of my work with various clients, many of them have asserted, "What happened to me (or my loved one) was just too horrible to forgive." Forgiveness doesn't mean you will forget what happened; it means you will remove the charge by releasing the emotional pain, which will allow you to consciously let go of the need to get even or receive compensation.

You might have scars, but you will no longer have open wounds. In order for you to create the beautiful life you want, you need to grieve what was lost and/or taken from you, and learn how to release those parts of your being that are stuck in darkness and pain. Light will illuminate the darkness. Forgiveness is the flame that lights the candle that illuminates the darkness.

While pain is a normal part of our human experience, suffering occurs when we cling to our pain and nurture our judgments. Learning to relinquish judgments – even toward those who have committed horribly cruel acts – increases our capacity for compassion and empathy, qualities that, I assure you, do not mean we become doormats. On the contrary, compassion and empathy pave the path to true inner peace and joy.

We do not relinquish judgments in order to become "good people." We relinquish them for the sake of our own inner peace, and by doing so, we become the best version of ourselves. Being angry and unforgiving actually increases the odds that you will attract and be triggered or upset by situations that mirror the original unforgivable act. This is a cycle that can repeat itself over and over again.

Acknowledging that we are all human and that we, at some point, may even have behaved cruelly toward another, is the first step toward true understanding. As Dr. George Pransky writes in, *The Relationship Handbook*, "The only way to eliminate harmful thoughts is through understanding."

I have found personally and for most of my clients, when we get to understanding, we open the doors to acceptance. The way to get there is through forgiveness. It will allow you to free stuck energy so that you will be able to create what you want, instead of reliving the past by constantly judging it and wishing it were different.

*"I learned a long time ago that some people would rather die than forgive. It's a strange truth, but forgiveness is a painful and difficult process. It's not something that happens overnight. It's an evolution of the heart."*
*—Sue Monk Kidd*

## Revenge Is Not the Answer

I first met Helena, a Holocaust survivor, in my neighborhood. She was leaving her yoga class when she noticed me sitting in my front garden writing. I just so happened to be writing about forgiveness…

She stopped and asked, "What are you writing?"

I said, "I'm writing about forgiveness. I've been working in the prison, and I'm taking notes."

She was startled but seemed intrigued and asked, "What do you do there?"

I explained my role there, and as I was talking about being able to sit with someone who had committed a terrible crime without judging them, she asked, "How do you do that? It seems impossible to me. I don't understand how you can be with criminals and not judge them."

I said, "I understand, but for some reason I'm able to sit with them and only see the human being who is thirsty for healing. I'm a channel for healing. Whether they deserve a second chance or not is not up to me. My work is different."

She started telling me that the only reason Hitler tried to annihilate the Jews was because Jews are superior. I asked, "How is that helping you?" When she didn't answer, I remarked, "Maybe nobody's superior or inferior; maybe we're just human beings doing different kinds of things."

She asked, "Why don't you believe that I'm better than the Nazis?"

I replied, "I'm not saying that I believe or don't believe. I'm saying that there are other options. Sometimes we go into denial and need to justify what happened to us, and that helps us move through life. Maybe this is the time to let that go."

Angrily, Helena replied, "You're just challenging me! How can you say that? What kind of person are you? You work to help people, and you don't see that Hitler was evil?!!"

Looking directly into her eyes with a soft, loving voice, I said, "Helena, I'm not saying that. In the big scheme of life, I don't know why Hitler happened." I paused and then continued with a different approach, "Did you ever read about the father whose daughter was kidnapped, abused and killed? It happened many years ago. Because of what happened to his daughter, he founded a nationwide organization to help support families who go through that kind of thing. I'm not saying that what happened to his daughter was good. What I'm saying is we don't know why things happen the way they do, or for what end. I'm just trying to suggest that using the superior or inferior justification might not be helping you at this moment."

She softened and said, "I'm interested in what you're saying."

I could see that a part of her was genuinely thirsty to understand forgiveness work, so I asked, "Would you be willing to work with me?"

During our first session, Helena declared, "I'm happy, I'm at peace, I go to yoga and I enjoy my life. I forgave the whole thing – the Holocaust – but I cannot forgive Hitler."

I asked, "Do you want to love?"

She declared, "Yes, of course, I want to love. I love the life I have… I love my son. What do you mean by that?"

I replied, "How can you really experience all that love has to offer if you can't forgive? If you don't forgive, you have hampered your ability to give and receive love."

She retorted, "I don't like the word 'forgiveness.' You're saying these things to me because you weren't there. You didn't experience it. So you can't tell me that I have to forgive."

I replied, "I'm not telling you that you have to forgive. You're telling me that you want to love, and I'm saying that in order to be able to really experience love, we have to be willing to forgive."

She replied firmly, "I already forgave. Do you think that if I hadn't forgiven, I could be at peace? I know that Hitler tried to obliterate us because we are better. Jews are better and smarter than others, and that's the only reason he wanted to obliterate us. I have come to accept that because we're better, we were targeted."

I responded, "Okay, explain to me what forgiveness is for you? What does that mean in your life?"

She said, "I'm at peace, and I accept and recognize that this happened to me because I am better."

"You're making a judgment."

She almost shouted, "What are you talking about – making a judgment?"

"Yes… in order to handle the truth and bear the reality of what happened, you qualify your 'forgiveness.' Every time I say forgiveness,

I experience your resistance. When you are in a state of resistance, you separate yourself from love, and yet you tell me that you want to experience love. What does forgiveness mean to you? Or should we call 'forgiveness' something else so you don't resist it?"

She said, "Forgiveness for me is imagining that even though it happened, it's not touching me anymore. I can be like the humming-bird just flying freely here and there. I'm free; it's not hurting me anymore."

I asked her, "Do you want revenge? What would you do to Hitler?"

She said without hesitation, "I would kill that motherfucker."

"Okay. So, do you think you have forgiven?"

She declared firmly without hesitation, "Yes!"

"Do you feel any satisfaction in getting even, in killing him?"

She thought about it for a minute and said reluctantly, "No... I don't want to do that. I don't want to experience that. I don't want humanity to go through that again, but I'm so much better than him. I would never have done that. How could God have permitted this to happen?"

I asked, "Are you willing to let go of the idea that everything is going to be fair?" Helena looked at me with confusion. I continued, "I came to the understanding at some point that God is not making people do things. Cruel actions are expressions of darkness, and the only thing that can dispel darkness is Light. Light comes from the divine within each person. It is God's gift to us, but God is not the one to blame. It's our responsibility to act according to the Light we have access to within."

I quoted something Dr. Martin Luther King, Jr. once said: "Dark-ness cannot drive out darkness: only light can do that. Hate cannot drive out hate: only love can do that."

Helena started sobbing, and when she looked at me, I could see her Soul through the ocean blue of her eyes. She asked, "Are you saying to me that I can access that light too?"

I could see that she had shifted into a higher level of consciousness. She was having a spontaneous experience of God within. She finally exclaimed that all her senses felt heightened. In that state of expanded awareness, radiant with God's Love, she sat crying softly, staring in awe at the trees, the birds and the sky.

With a reverential tone, she whispered, "I think I'm ready to let this go. I don't need to feel superior to justify forgiving."

Letting go of this judgment had nothing to do with condoning anything Hitler had done. The judgment of superiority had been a "crutch" that allowed Helena to feel as though she had forgiven Hitler and the Nazis when she really had not. When she let go of the *need* for that judgment, it was a huge relief.

People sometimes do horrific things based on the level of consciousness they have at that moment. I will say one more time that forgiving doesn't mean condoning. The reality is that forgiving horrific acts doesn't mean they won't occur again, but revenge just continues to perpetuate the cycle of violence.

By forgiving, you take action in the direction that creates more love and understanding in the world, which may ultimately cause a positive change. That change may come slowly, but at least forgiving does not add more combustible material to the fire. Unconditional forgiveness never needs justification.

## God Consciousness and Forgiveness

The phenomenon of a client shifting into God Consciousness has happened many times in my sessions, most specifically when we are working on forgiveness. Forgiveness is not just a gesture or thought or belief or emotion, it is Divine Energy at work. When we are able to rise above our own personal hurts and see ourselves and all human beings with the compassion of God, we are able to forgive and accept anything, not because cruelty is okay, but because we are all One.

All the various manifestations of God's expression here on Earth are for our learning and growth. As we expand in consciousness through forgiveness and acceptance, we are able to move into love and compassion. We become the Living Light, dispelling darkness wherever it exists just by being.

> *"We must develop and maintain the capacity to forgive. He who is devoid of the power to forgive is devoid of the power to love. There is some good in the worst of us and some evil in the best of us. When we discover this, we are less prone to hate our enemies."*
> —Martin Luther King, Jr.

## Unconditional Love Requires Unconditional Forgiveness

Helena said she wanted to take a break to thoroughly ponder everything she'd discussed with me. After several months, we continued with the sessions, and she confessed that she was still fighting with herself to shift her sense of superiority. She recounted several instances in which she had become enraged at what she felt was another person's incompetency. She characterized these incompetent or unprofessional people as inferior.

In a very gentle way, I asked, "Do you think you really are superior to these people?"

She replied, "Maybe… yes. I've been dealing with people who don't know what they're doing, yet they're in positions of power, and I'm frustrated!"

"Whatever this incompetent person is doing may not be very professional, but does that mean he is your inferior? Maybe it's just that in this area, he's not performing well. Inside yourself, you are categorizing these people you deem inferior as second-class citizens. You are diminishing them. If a person were to take those thoughts to the extreme, what would happen?"

She opened her eyes wide, looked at me aghast and asked, "Are you telling me that I'm like Hitler?"

I replied calmly, "I'm not telling you anything… How does that feel inside of you?"

She started crying and then laughing. She said, "So I'm doing the same thing. I'm doing the same thing."

"You aren't taking extreme action, but inside of yourself, you are judging others in the same way.

"Are you telling me that it's okay whatever they do?"

"No, it's not okay whatever they do… You can file a complaint or talk to them, but the fact that they are doing their job in a way that doesn't meet your standards doesn't mean they're inferior, or that they deserve to be punished or have their rights taken away."

On my recommendation, she started observing herself in situations where she felt the need to put on her superiority mask. When feelings of superiority came up, I encouraged her not to react, but to just experience and accept her feelings.

She said this process helped her, but that she was still a work in progress… (*Aren't we all?*) Sometimes she got angry and righteous, and sometimes she just laughed at herself. When she was able to feel more accepting of herself, she was generally able to feel more accepting of the person or situation that was causing her reaction. In those instances, she said she had been able to deal with the situation with more equanimity and compassion.

I encouraged Helena to start a "learning journal." She had to write in her journal every day about an experience related to her feeling inferior and/or superior, and then rate her experience as either upsetting (qualifying the kind of upset she felt – anger, irritation, frustration, sadness etc.) or non-impactful. After several weeks, we read her journal without judging it. It was a powerful exercise, and she started experiencing subtle changes in the way she perceived people, including herself.

I explained to her, "If you want to experience unconditional love, you must also experience unconditional forgiveness. You don't need a reason to forgive. Then again, maybe the only reason you forgive is to be at peace with yourself and to experience love. Maybe this is being selfish because you're doing it for yourself. You cannot change the world by nurturing your hatred for Hitler, but you can change the world if you love yourself and leave that as your legacy."

*"Free the mind from all disturbing thoughts*
*and fill it with love and joy."*
—Paramahansa Yogananda

## Forgiving God and Acknowledging the Light Within

I had not anticipated that I would have the opportunity to go back to the prison to continue my work with Johnny and the other inmates, but the group of volunteers I worked with and I were able to get the prison to agree to sponsor us for another weekend workshop. During the months between my first and second visits, I had been corresponding regularly with Johnny, who was making tremendous progress, but was anxious to address his feelings of resentment toward his mother.

He was still working on self-forgiveness and had gotten to a place where he was able to offer love and inspiration to others who were going through different stages in their own healing. But he was troubled by the feelings that had surfaced toward his mother and her part in the molestation he had experienced at the hands of his stepfather. For about three years, from the time he was six years old, Johnny's stepfather sexually abused him. To keep him quiet, his stepfather would threaten, "If you say anything to anyone, I'll kill you."

Johnny said to me, "My mother should have known what kind of man she married. She should have taken care of me… she wasn't a good mom. I felt abandoned by her, by life, and… by God." Johnny felt betrayed by the person who was supposed to love and protect him. On some level, his resentment toward his mother was greater than the pain he'd experienced at the hands of his stepfather. Johnny wondered how he would ever be able to forgive her, the one who was supposed to protect him. He felt she was even worse than his stepfather.

Johnny explained, "I have forgiven my stepfather. I understand that men can feel disempowered and behave in cruel ways… I understand that, but how can I forgive my mother for putting me in that position, for not taking care of me? If she had protected me, I wouldn't have killed my fiancée. I destroyed a life. I was jealous. I thought my fiancée didn't love me, that she was betraying me… I didn't want to kill her but I had the gun next to me and I did it. I did it! I can't go back, I can't change that…"

I asked him, "Can you remember what you felt like when your fiancée came home from the bar?"

"I felt betrayed."

"Yes," I said gently. "What else?"

He paused for a few minutes and then said, "Abandoned. I was afraid she was going to abandon me... that I wasn't good enough."

"Was that feeling new?"

Something happened inside of Johnny at that moment. He realized he'd resented his mother his entire life for betraying and abandoning him. He suddenly understood that his rage wasn't just about his fiancée. He'd "killed" his feelings of being betrayed and abandoned by his mother, life and God.

Between the two visits, I had sent Johnny a children's fable by Neale Donald Walsch called *The Little Soul and the Sun*. Paraphrasing, I recounted the part of the story where the Little Soul says to God that she wants to learn about forgiveness:

*"God says, 'There is no one to forgive... Everything I have made is perfect.' The Little Soul won't accept this explanation and insists that she wants to learn about forgiveness, so the Friendly Soul steps forward and volunteers to be the 'bad one' in their next lifetime together so that the Little Soul has the opportunity to learn about forgiveness. The Little Soul is ecstatic. The Friendly Soul is happy to oblige, but cautions that they may both forget who they really are when the Friendly Soul does the worst thing to the Little Soul that she could possibly ever imagine. The Little Soul promises that she will remember who they **really** are – that they are the Light – and will thank that incarnation of the Friendly Soul for bringing her the opportunity to be the Forgiving One, '...the chance to experience myself as Who I Am.'"*

After recounting this part of the story to Johnny, I asked, "What if that's why you came here – to learn how to forgive? There's nothing that God cannot forgive, and if we have God inside of us, that means you have the opportunity to transform your pain into something positive for yourself and others."

At the end of our time together, I encouraged Johnny to make the forgiveness work his spiritual practice. I counseled him to stop analyzing whether or not it was working, but to just do it. I said that one day something would click inside, and the doors of his own heaven would be fully open. I encouraged him to include God in his forgiveness work. I explained that letting go of all the judgments we've placed on God and forgiving ourselves for making those judgments is the path to real freedom.

He thanked me and told me that his intention was to keep doing the work and that when released, he wanted to offer his life in service to kids who have gone through sexual and physical abuse. He sensed that he had the opportunity to experience redemption through his loving service.

> *"Forgiveness says you are given another chance*
> *to make a new beginning."*
> —Desmond Tutu

## Reflective Questions on Forgiving the Unforgivable

Ask yourself the following questions, and allow the first answer that pops into your head to be the answer you write down. I encourage you to accept whatever comes forward and use this tool as an opportunity to discover the places inside yourself where you are still suffering:

1. If I forgive the person who hurt me, am I condoning what he/she said/did? Are they going to receive punishment? Will justice prevail?

2. If I let go of my anger at the person who hurt me or the situation that humiliated me, will I commit the same mistake again?

3. If I let go of my anger, will I be allowing the person who hurt me back into my life?

4. Does my anger make me feel safe, protected?

5. If I let go of my anger, will I be inviting the person who hurt me once to hurt me again?

6. Do I feel lost without my anger, without my story about how I was wronged, hurt, used or abused?

7. Do I feel justified in my anger? Righteous? Right? On the side of "good"?

## Gentle Coaching
## on Forgiving the Unforgivable

Here is how I would begin to engage you if you answered YES to any of the above questions:

1. If I forgive the person who hurt me, am I condoning what he/she said/did? Are they going to receive punishment? Will justice prevail?

   **Remember that Forgiveness is for you, not them. It is a gift you give yourself. It sets you free. It is not up to you to take justice into your own hands; it will only cause more pain and suffering, and you will then become the perpetrator.**

2. If I let go of my anger at the person who hurt me or the situation that humiliated me, will I commit the same mistake again?

   This is a mistaken belief. Your anger has nothing to do with keeping you from committing the same mistake. If anything, your anger may be attracting situations and people that continue to test your boundaries.

3. If I let go of my anger, will I be allowing the person who hurt me back into my life?

   Your anger assures you that this person is constantly in your life through your obsessive thinking about them, or because you are expending energy to suppress your thoughts about them. Forgiveness doesn't mean you must reconcile.

4. Does my anger make me feel safe, protected?

   This is false protection. Your anger continues to make you vulnerable to circumstances that will mirror the situation that hurt you in the first place.

5. If I let go of my anger, will I be inviting the person who hurt me once to hurt me again?

   Being angry and unforgiving actually increases the odds of you being triggered emotionally by something else that they do. You will keep repeating the same cycle again and again.

6. Do I feel lost without my anger, without my story about how I was wronged, hurt, used or abused?

   If you let go of your story, you would not be the same person who holds a grudge, lives in fear and needs a wall up to protect yourself. Fear separates you from love, and love is who you really are. Drop your story and experience your loving essence. Your heart is already open, which is what you will experience as the walls that you have built to "protect yourself from hurt" come tumbling down.

7. Do I feel justified in my anger? Righteous? Right? On the side of "good"?

   **Justifying your continued outrage toward major injustices such as murder, genocide and violent crime (as opposed to "petty concerns" like not being invited to a party), does not make you righteous or on the side of "right." Your "righteousness" simply makes you an angry person, stuck in your pain. Forgiveness gives us a "clean slate," another chance to live again.**

Before moving forward, give yourself some quiet time to reflect on these questions and my responses. Then ask yourself, "What am I aware of because of this issue?" In your answer might reside your lesson.

Always keep in mind that by not forgiving the unforgivable, you keep yourself in jail. You are the jailor and the prisoner! You deny yourself the opportunity to experience inner and sometimes outer freedom. When you forgive, you serve the world from your heart, not your wound. Ask yourself, "Who would I be if I forgave the unforgivable? How would I feel?" From that place, you can experience your divine essence, the truth of who you really are – the free soul who has let go of the hurts and of the ego.

> *"As I walked out the door toward the gate that would lead to my freedom, I knew if I didn't leave my bitterness and hatred behind, I'd still be in prison."*
> —Nelson Mandela

❖ ❖ ❖

# CHAPTER FIVE

# HAPPINESS, FREEDOM AND FORGIVENESS

*"Happiness is when what you think, what you say, and what you do are in harmony."*
—Mahatma Gandhi

## Your Internal GPS

We all know what a GPS is: "The **Global Positioning System (GPS)** is a space-based navigation system that provides location and time information in all weather conditions, anywhere on or near the Earth…" (Wikipedia)

When we are finally able to touch freedom and happiness, those experiences become like an internal "GPS" or touchstone that we can access again and again when we veer off the path. Whenever we feel derailed by old hurts that rise from the depths, or by new hurts that take us by surprise, that GPS is available to lead us back to the path of peace, freedom, happiness and love. The most direct route you can take is the one that is paved with forgiveness.

For me, forgiveness is the tool that allowed me to relate to my husband from the heart and not the hurt. It is difficult for us as human beings to let go of anger, hurt and fear, so that we can embrace forgiveness, happiness and freedom. It seems at times that it's easier to hold on to anger than it is to let go and embrace the Light within.

When we experience emotional pain, we are left with a wound that needs to be healed. If the wound remains open without healing, we relate to everything in the world from that wound. In a sense, we want the perpetrator, the person who caused us pain, to pay. We want to get even, and only then will we be persuaded to move on. But really, what "payment" do we want to receive? How will they pay us back? The open wound acts like a poorly calibrated GPS that leads us directly toward what we don't want to experience. It's like trying not to hit a hole in the road when riding a bicycle. The more afraid you are of the hole, the more likely you are to hit it. Fear can be quite a magnet!

## Ending the Cycle of Pain

When we walk out into the world relating from our wounds, we answer life's experience with resentment and distortion rather than understanding. We try to cover up the pain by applying bandages to the wound. But it's like putting a bandage on a nail in your foot. Until you remove the nail, the pain will continue and ultimately become infected.

Have you ever poured salt on an open wound? Ouch! That is the feeling we have when we relate from the hurt. The pain escalates. We sometimes don't even know why we end up in an argument or react with anger. The child inside of us who experienced the pain is still hurting, and when something happens to trigger that pain, we react in a way that may be out of proportion to the actual event. We've all experienced this – it's very human. Yet, it's embarrassing, isn't it? And it can even get us into trouble or cause a relationship to end forever. The solution is working through that pain, and forgiveness must be at the center of that work.

In order to relate from the heart, we need to transform the open wound into a healed scar. We will remember what happened, but the wound will be allowed to close. The nail will be extracted, the infection will clear, and the pain will be gone. The wound cannot be healed, though, until we let go of the illusion that the past could have been different. It has already happened and cannot be changed. We must accept our own humanness and the humanness of others. We all sometimes "miss the mark" and fail to live up to our expectations. In some cases, a human being has been so deeply damaged that he or she commits acts that are beyond our comprehension.

As Jesus said in Luke 23:34: "...forgive them, for they do not know what they are doing." That phrase has meant a lot to me in my life. It helped me understand that whatever someone else does "to" me isn't about me. It's about their own inner pain and lack of awareness. I also realized that when I've made mistakes, it wasn't about anyone else. It was about my own unresolved issues. My husband's infidelity was a result of his own emotional issues. It wasn't about me.

Tracy realized that, too. When she was able to understand that her husband's actions came out of his own insecurity, forgiveness was easier for her. She even discovered that the painful situation was a kind of miracle in disguise. It was a miracle that helped her open her eyes and heart. It changed her perspective and helped her grow into a wiser, more psychologically and spiritually healthy person.

I know now that we are all doing the best we can from the level of consciousness we have at the time of our actions. Hitler's well-documented painful childhood is not in any way a justification for his actions, but it is a possible, at least partial, explanation. Certainly, few of us have such radically destructive reactions to painful childhoods, but it has been shown that serial killers and sociopaths have often suffered through abusive childhoods.

Unless we are able to reach a place of forgiveness, the cycles of pain, anger and violence are in danger of continuing. When we are able to surrender to unconditional forgiveness, we have the capacity to live beautiful lives of freedom, happiness, harmony and love.

## Joseph Uncovers the God Within

How does forgiveness relate to happiness and freedom? Are happiness and freedom even possible without forgiveness? Joseph believed that he was "doomed" to live a life without the experience of happiness. He did what he was "supposed" to do because he was a kind, responsible man. He had good manners, he worked hard and he honored his family obligations.

He would smile, but rarely laughed. There was no enthusiasm or passion in his life. Enthusiasm comes from the Greek word entheos (divinely inspired or possessed by a god), so you could say that Joseph had lost his connection to the god within – his inspiration. He had to work hard to keep a big part of himself from his consciousness, and this kept him feeling separated from his essence. Though he wasn't aware of it, the child within him was terrified of remembering what had happened to him, so the only way for him to survive was to disconnect. All that was left of his former self was a dim light that flickered somewhere deep inside of him.

However, no matter how hard Joseph tried to hide what he was feeling, it came through. Even though his wife didn't know what was going on inside of him, she recognized that something wasn't right. The pain of living with someone in that state was definitely challenging.

As Joseph and I worked together, he was able to unearth his traumatic memories. It certainly did not happen overnight, but in time, he was able to heal the experiences in his past by letting go of his anger, pain and sadness. This allowed him to move into acceptance and forgiveness of his perpetrators as well as himself. As a result, little by little, the dim light inside him became stronger.

Joseph had been victimized as a child, and as an adult, became the victim of his own thoughts and fears. An important step for him was changing his thoughts. Doing so helped him alter his emotions and rewire his brain to focus on acceptance, forgiveness, gratitude, freedom, peace, and eventually, joy and happiness.

One day I said to Joseph, "You don't need to believe everything you think."

He looked at me like I was saying something incoherent and asked, "What do you mean by that?"

I countered with, "What made you keep your silence through all these years?"

"Because I was told to do so! I was told not to open my mouth, that whatever happened never happened!"

I could see he was starting to feel anxious. His breathing was labored, and he was making faces and clenching his fists. His face showed the pain he had been carrying for so long.

I asked him, "Did you think that by keeping that secret you were safe?"

"Yes!"

"What else did you think?"

He didn't want to answer me, but he finally replied, "I thought I was keeping the promise I made… Nobody had to know. I thought that if nobody knew, nobody was going to make fun of me."

I asked, "What did you make out of that?"

"I don't know," he said with tears in his eyes. "I thought that if nobody knew, nothing happened, and if nothing happened, I could be a normal kid again."

"Did you believe that, Joseph?" I asked softly.

"Yes, I did believe it… but it didn't help."

"You see, Joseph? We don't need to believe everything we think. The vow you made under such a shock made you live your life in the shadows. If you change the thought, how do you feel? If you understand that you don't have to believe everything you think, or run your life according to something you thought when you were a little child who experienced a deeply traumatic event, you can be…"

"Free!" he said with a big sigh.

Ultimately, forgiveness dissolved the barriers that Joseph had built to protect himself. He found that daily forgiveness of the "little things" he called "stones in the middle of his path to happiness" had a ripple effect in his life. The more he worked on forgiveness in this way, the more he felt empowered to make positive choices that led him to experience greater degrees of happiness and peace.

Even as I write this, Joseph and I are working on letting go of more sadness and pain, and there are times when he still finds himself resisting happiness. The ego doesn't think it's safe for us to feel free or happy. As Joseph has become more aware of this resistance, he has been able to release it more often.

As he has said to me, "You know Clara, my first answer most of the time is 'NO.' Sometimes I just have to say 'no' to say no, and then I say 'yes' to myself, say 'yes' to happiness, to laughter…"

Joseph wore many coats in order to prevent his heart from being hurt again. Revealing his feelings was scary at first, but ultimately fruitful. As he began to feel the warmth of his own being and his own authenticity, he was able to shed the coats. He no longer felt the need to protect himself.

"Forgiveness has been like oxygen inside of me, like really breathing life," he explained to me.

Feelings of despair and separation are present when you are not connecting to who you really are. When you don't feel God, your higher source within, you don't feel the Soul. When you don't feel the Soul, the Spirit, you might do anything to feel something. The process of forgiveness will pull back the veil that is preventing you from seeing and feeling who you really are, your essence. When you reconnect with your essence, the fire within – or enthusiasm – is reignited.

For Joseph, happiness has become possible on a moment-by-moment basis through forgiveness, which allows him to keep dissolving the layers that have separated him from his enthusiasm – the god within.

*"Most people are about as happy*
*as they make up their minds to be."*
—Abraham Lincoln

## Happiness and Freedom Are Choices

Johnny showed me that happiness and freedom are more about what is happening inside of us than outside. Yes, he was literally a prisoner without external freedom, but more than that, he was a prisoner of his own thought patterns.

"In order to experience inner freedom, we need to experience a free heart," I said to Johnny.

"How do I do that?" he shouted in frustration.

Forgiving himself for the crime he had committed, as well as forgiving himself and his perpetrators for what happened to him as a child, initiated a process that eventually allowed him to detach from how he had defined himself. He finally came to understand that he was not his past or the labels he had given himself.

Then and only then was he empowered to experience feelings of hope. He could disengage from his negative self-talk because he had separated himself from those thoughts. He was *having* thoughts, but the thoughts were not necessarily the truth. And though he was *having* feelings, he *wasn't* his feelings. Johnny learned that emotions are just passing visitors; they aren't who we are. Actually, emotions are thoughts experienced physiologically. It's as simple as that.

> *"The happiness of your thoughts depends*
> *on the quality of your thoughts."*
> —Marcus Aurelius

This poem by Rumi illuminates the importance of accepting our emotions. In embracing and welcoming them with awareness rather than fearing them, we have the opportunity to help them pass through as the guests they are. When we identify with them and hold on to them, they become permanent unwelcome residents in the "house" of the mind.

## The Guest House

This being human is a guest house.
Every morning a new arrival.

A joy, a depression, a meanness,
some momentary awareness comes
as an unexpected visitor.

Welcome and entertain them all!
Even if they are a crowd of sorrows,
who violently sweep your house
empty of its furniture,
still, treat each guest honorably.
He may be clearing you out
for some new delight.

The dark thought, the shame, the malice,
meet them at the door laughing and invite them in.

Be grateful for whatever comes
because each has been sent
as a guide from beyond.

Gradually, Johnny's judgments and negative thoughts became less pervasive. Since those thoughts were what triggered his emotional suffering, releasing them allowed him to begin to feel free inside. In a sense, Johnny experienced greater freedom in his prison cell than many people in the outside world who remain victimized by their own thoughts day in and day out.

Happiness and freedom are choices. We have the power to choose them if we learn the tools for doing so. We can live in the drama, or we can do the deep inner work to dissolve the barriers that separate us from happiness. We are the ones who hold the keys to our inner peace and freedom.

## Relating from the Heart, Not the Hurt

Rather than stay attached to what happened between my husband and the other woman, which would have kept me in a state of misery, I did the work to process through it – thoroughly. Practicing forgiveness allowed me to move on from feeling betrayed. I was eventually able to relate to my husband *from the heart, not the hurt*, and make decisions about our future from a place of compassion rather than anger.

I established a relationship with my husband's son from the very beginning, and I made sure I was relating to him from my heart, not a place of duty or victimhood. I was able to do this by applying the 3Fs process on a continual basis. As a result of this, I was able to experience peace and freedom amidst this turmoil in our lives. Using and introducing my husband to this process allowed us to experience compassion for each other and accept what each of us was going through. In fact, we actually experienced a kind of resurrection as a couple.

> *"Let the brain go to work, let it meet the heart,*
> *and you will be able to forgive."*
> —Maya Angelou

## Misinterpretation of Reality

One of the ways that we can release barriers to happiness and freedom is by evaluating our interpretations of reality. We often tell ourselves stories about who we are and what the events in our lives mean. We assume these stories are true, but most of the time they're simply our interpretations based on pain, hurt, anger and what we've been taught, consciously or unconsciously, by our parents, our culture and community.

One of the reasons that childhood pain is so pervasive is that we have even less of a capacity for interpreting events accurately when we're children. The assumptions we make stay with us unless and until we challenge them in adulthood. This is what happened to both Joseph and Johnny. They told themselves stories about their abuse that had no basis in reality, and those stories caused them immense pain throughout their lives.

Only when they brought their assumptions into consciousness in adulthood were they able to see the misperceptions in their thinking. I have been working with this concept in my own life as well. For example, for many years, I thought of myself as responsible for the happiness and well-being of the people I love. This stemmed from a misinterpretation I held about responsibility – a false idea that I think many people hold. I have found through the years, working with people from all walks of life, that many of them believed that part of their job description in life was to make their loved ones happy.

Because of what we experienced as children, we believe we aren't safe unless we are responsible for everyone, unless we're "perfect" – whatever that means for each of us. We try so hard to live up to the expectations of others because we desire to be loved and believe that by making others happy, we will be deserving of their love, and ultimately happiness.

Like so many of us, I misunderstood what it meant to be a "good girl." I just knew that I shouldn't feel or express anger. I felt I had to be the responsible one at all costs. In order to be worthy of my parents' love, to make them proud, I had to be perfect. I decided I would be available and kind, and I would take care of everyone's needs and happiness. It worked out perfectly for a while until at some point I realized that I was leaving myself out.

Shortly after finding out about my husband's affair, and his son, I had the thought, "I hate sex." I remembered all the emotional pain I'd experienced around sex, and I thought about all of the reports I'd seen about rape throughout the world. It was easy to see sex as an evil, but it was also clear to me that this was not about sex.

Sex is a tool, and how we use it determines our experience. Do we use it to show need? To ask for love? To release anger? At that time, it was easy for me to blame my feelings on sex. As I worked through my process, I had to acknowledge that sex is a wonderful thing and was not to blame for the pain I felt. My pain was all about my issues and how I related to sex.

How many of us have a complicated relationship with sexuality? The 3Fs process helped me heal my misinterpretations. I consciously released the punishment patterns I had created in my mind related to sex and perfection. By releasing judgments about sex and my own striving for perfection, I made way for experiencing greater degrees of inner freedom and happiness in my life.

As a result, I am now free to experience and enjoy. I have made a conscious decision to liberate my unconscious from my false beliefs. As author David R. Hawkins puts it: "What is life, in and of itself? ... It is the color of the glasses we put on. If we put on gray glasses coming from Grief, then everything looks sad.... If we have fear-colored glasses, everything looks like fear."

Every day, I ask myself, "What kind of day do I want to have?" If the glasses I see next to my night table are fear/worry glasses, I consciously say "no" and make the choice to pick a different pair. However, I'd like to clarify that it's perfectly fine to "wear gray glasses" when you are mourning or legitimately sad and need to cry or grieve. But you might consider – after having processed your emotions – donning pink, red or green glasses to support a shift out of sadness and grief into joy, acceptance, equanimity and peace.

## Freedom from Limiting Interpretations of Reality

If we want to empower ourselves, we need to ask ourselves, "What do I believe about this situation? What are my judgments about this? What story am I telling myself about this? And is it true?" Answering these questions honestly frees us from the limiting beliefs that cause us suffering. We can then "update" our software, replacing the "pain code" with the "empowerment code."

Ultimate freedom comes from our true self, not from the fake self that has been created as a result of our irrational beliefs. Ultimate freedom comes from empowering ourselves by becoming aware of those beliefs and letting go of judgments through the process of forgiveness.

This awareness can work in simple situations, such as when you feel upset because a friend hasn't called when she said she would. Think of all the assumptions you might make in a circumstance like that. I might assume that she was rejecting me or upset with me, or that I had done something wrong. I might judge *her* for being inconsiderate or disorganized. When I stop myself from making assumptions and judgments for her "mistake," I avoid a lot of unnecessary drama and the potential for the loss of a friendship over something inconsequential.

Let's say a friend of yours reacted in anger to something you said that you thought was just an innocent remark. You inadvertently triggered this friend to re-experience some hurt that you had no way of knowing was there. You could see the situation from your own hurt, or you could see that your friend lost control of her emotions due to some wound from her past. Hasn't that happened to you at some point in your life?

This is one way you can reframe a circumstance and see it from a more compassionate viewpoint. You can honor your own hurt feelings without reacting defensively like your friend, and in so doing, you can change the energy so that the hurts don't escalate and threaten your relationship.

## Privacy vs. Secrecy

When we hide something, it's usually because we are ashamed of it. We don't want others to find out about it. For example, Joseph kept the abuse he suffered hidden. It was his "dark" secret, and it took a lot of energy for him to hold on to that secret. He almost killed himself keeping it hidden. It was his mistaken beliefs about what had happened to him that caused him to believe he had to keep it secret.

Secrecy differs from privacy, however. Unlike secrecy, privacy empowers us. When I learned about my husband's son, I didn't want to keep it secret. I wanted to bring light to that secret, but that didn't mean I was going to write a press release about it! Privacy means that

I have the right to tell only the people I choose. For Joseph, telling me about his secret empowered him because I was a safe person for him to confide in. He is under no obligation to tell anyone else in his life right now.

A few weeks after I learned about my husband's son, I sent a letter to our closest family members communicating the news. I asked for the privacy to deal with it in our own time without drama or judgments. When we go through crises, we can allow ourselves to be drawn into the abyss of shame by hiding our pain, or we can heal our pain by disclosing our feelings and the details of the situation to people who are worthy of our trust.

I transformed a dark secret into a private matter that became public after I took the time to heal. When I decided it was time to reveal the truth to the rest of my family, I used that energy to heal instead of using up my energy to maintain the façade. I couldn't control what the members of my family were going to say or do, but I knew that I wanted to respond with love. When we forgive, we are not only freeing ourselves, we are also healing the generations to come. Each of us has our own pace and timing. Even though my healing happened relatively quickly, there is no right or wrong timing. It is important to respect the dignity of each person's process.

Recently, my husband and I were in Argentina in the city where his son lives. We went out to dinner with him and had a good time. I experienced such grace that I told this young man I loved him and that my heart was open to him.

My husband asked me later that night, "How do you do it?"

I showed him an old scar I have on my arm, and I said, "This is a scar. It's healed. I can pour salt on it, and I won't feel anything. This is the same thing. I have accepted. That doesn't mean I wouldn't have liked things to be different. But does it really help to focus on that? Some days have been easier than others, but the scar has healed." Forgiveness was the healing agent.

## The "Happiness Contract"

Most people grow up without consciously knowing that they have a "happiness (or unhappiness) contract." We unconsciously assimilate the degree to which we are allowed to be happy from our parents, our culture, and our own experiences in life. We also unconsciously absorb from our parents and our culture "forgiveness agreements" – how and whom we are allowed to forgive.

Sometimes people want to forgive and let go, but being part of a community that experienced trauma and suffering makes it more difficult. We have an internal sense that if we belong to a culture and/ or a family that has experienced pain, letting go and forgiving – the perpetrators, the past, the circumstances, etc. – is a kind of betrayal.

I had a client named Licia who wanted to renew a relationship with the father who had once abandoned her and her family. He showed up one night at her family home ten long years after he'd left. Licia could not believe that the man standing outside the door was the same man she'd seen for the last time on a cold night in winter ten years earlier.

She told me that for months after he left when she was a child, she cried every night until she finally fell asleep. She saw him in her dreams for many years, until she eventually gave up on the expectation that he would one day come home. She had long since ceased dreaming of his return, but there he was, standing on her front porch, waiting for her to react.

Licia told me, "I couldn't believe the man in front of me was actually my father. I had been so upset with him my whole life... The last time I saw him, I was 11 years old, and my image of him, my memory of him, was so different from the man before me. He wasn't as old as I remembered him to be. He looked like he had not been in the sun for a long time. He was very pale. When he disappeared from our lives, life was tough. Not much time for laughs. Mom had to take an extra job to be able to make ends meet. Each of us had to help in the house, and we had chores. Sundays we went to church, but in the afternoons we had a little play time before we had to get ready for school the next day."

She continued with her story: "My older brother, who carried our father's name, started having behavioral problems. My three younger sisters had to be taken care of. All of a sudden, there he was, the cause of our family's destruction and despair, standing in front of me! His face didn't show the passing of time, although his beautiful blue eyes had wrinkles around them and showed deep sorrow. I noticed that his emotions wouldn't let him speak clearly. The halting words he spoke will be with me forever."

He said, "Licia, please forgive me."

Licia wanted desperately to forgive him so that they could have a real connection. But session after session she said, "I want to forgive him, but I can't. My mother doesn't deserve this pain, and my sisters would never talk to me again."

She felt that if she forgave him, she would be betraying her family and their unspoken agreement to shut him out the way he had shut them out. She felt that if she forgave him, nothing her family had done to survive his abandonment would count.

How many times have you wanted to claim happiness but stopped yourself because your internal monitor warned you that it was not allowed, or that it was false, or undeserved, or would be disappointing, or might even be too much? We measure the amount of happiness we are allowed to experience according to what our parents taught us, according to their own life experiences, as well as our own.

Sometimes we feel guilty if we are too happy; it's easier to suppress our happiness and live in the dullness of our familiar pain. This is the pain you, your family and culture have "agreed" is appropriate. What is meant to be punishment for the perpetrator or abuser ends up being a kind of permanent punishment for the one living in a state of suffering.

If you truly want to be happy, revisit how your family and culture relate to forgiveness, and then to happiness. After you have done that, be willing to rewrite your own contract… one that will set you free!

## Get Happy Now!

Many experts believe that happiness is a state of mind. It is true that a life without troubles can make us happy. When we have prosperity and a great love life, for instance, we experience happiness – but it's also true that this is a "conditioned" response.

What happens to your mood if you lose your job, don't feel financially secure, or go through a painful divorce? Do you feel low? Does it mean you are doomed to be unhappy?

No, of course it doesn't. And that's the point: Being a happy person does NOT depend on the circumstances of your life. Happiness is something you can feel regardless of the state of your finances or your marriage. If you learn to turn to a place inside yourself that is filled with love no matter what's happening in your lives, you can then experience happiness even during sad or stressful moments.

Try this exercise: Think about what's usually happening when you feel great – are you playing with your children or grandkids? Or perhaps you feel happiest when you're teaching them something you know will serve them later in life. Maybe happiness comes when you create something with your hands, or volunteer at a hunger center, or do something you've never done before.

Think about those times, and "record" the feelings and situations in your mind. Then, the next time you are not happy, ask yourself, "What am I attached to in this unhappy place that I can release?" Let go of it, and envision your happy times instead. It takes a little practice, but this simple exercise can work miracles and change your outlook, even when you're going through very rough times.

Another simple but powerful thing you can do when you're feeling low is to focus on gratitude. I've experienced tremendous feelings of empowerment during the most challenging times in my life because I was able to feel gratitude for what I was learning in those moments. Pulling up that feeling of gratitude in such times changes your whole perspective – it certainly has changed mine – and you see a shift in the whole dynamic that operates in your life. It has been liberating for me, and you will see that feeling genuine gratitude can be liberating for you, too.

I encourage my clients to keep a "gratitude journal," where they write down five things every day for which they are grateful. It's a good practice, and if you write in your gratitude journal each morning, it helps you to start your day on a cheerier note and makes it easier to "condition" yourself to think positively on rough days.

Two noted psychologists, David Myers and Ed Diener (who specialize in happiness research), have said, "Happiness grows less from the passive experience of desirable circumstances than from involvement in valued activities and progress toward one's goals." What they're saying is, we find happiness by doing things we love and working toward personal goals that are important to us.

Those goals can be as simple as treating people well. Another inspirational author, John Rogers, gives us a beautiful quote: "Love is the healer, joy is the expression." When you find yourself in an unhappy place, ask yourself, "Where can I apply more love? Do I need to behave in a more loving way in my relationships? Should I practice more acceptance? Or should I love myself more?"

Determining the extent of your own happiness is fairly easy. Just divide a sheet of paper into four columns, listing the things you think, say and do for a couple of days. The fourth column is for your reflections and comments as you go along. What do your lists tell you? Are you happy? If not, what can you do to balance those three areas? Being in balance helps you to feel more energetic and happy.

To paraphrase Albert Einstein, we cannot keep doing the same things over and over and expect different results. If you have not experienced freedom or happiness in your life, maybe it's time to give forgiveness a try. Forgiveness is to happiness as breath is to life. Forgiveness of everything and everyone, including ourselves, dissolves the barriers that prevent us from experiencing happiness.

✦ ✦ ✦

# CHAPTER SIX

# FORGIVENESS AND HEALTH

*"...forgiveness is an absolute necessity*
*for continued human existence."*
*—Archbishop Desmond Tutu*

I was preparing a lecture entitled, "Leadership and Conflict in the Workplace," that I had been asked to present to a group of executives, when out of the blue I experienced an acute pain in my stomach, like someone had punched me. I diligently tried to finish my work, but I was not feeling well. So I had to stop writing, reschedule one of my clients (something I rarely do), and go home to bed.

A day of detox and rest helped, and I was again ready to work on my lecture. It was just a few days before I was supposed to present it, so I was working hard to complete it when I received an email from the organization who'd hired me to give the lecture. It said that someone else had been chosen to give the lecture. Once again, I felt the punch in the stomach. Although I knew it was "politics" and not anything about me that had made them change their minds at the last minute, I felt betrayed.

While I pondered the situation, I did what I know best: I went through the 3Fs process. I first allowed myself to express my frustration and acknowledge the fear I was experiencing. The fear that I was losing an opportunity to do what I loved triggered my pain and emotions even more intensely. I tasted the bitterness of betrayal, and I knew I had more work to do. That wound was still open and was bringing up the memories of other wounds. Even though this was "real," I knew that the original wounds were coming to the surface.

A week later, I woke up in the night with a pain in the left side of my stomach that made it hard for me to move or walk. My husband offered to drive me to the emergency room, but I said I wanted to wait. I spent a couple of days in bed as the pain slowly subsided. My husband kept insisting that I go to the doctor.

"Don't be stubborn!" he admonished. "Do you think you're going to heal yourself?"

"I'm not going to 'cure' myself," I explained, "but my body is giving me messages."

It was screaming at me, and I wanted to hear, to really get what it was saying to me. The first two days I lay in bed, I barely ate, and I didn't move much. I meditated and prayed. In the silence, I asked God to speak to me through my body. Tears of old pain were washing away the memories, old betrayals and my own betrayals. The idea that I had to digest so much pain was being released. I understood that the judgments I was still holding toward painful situations from my past were "stuck" inside of me. I knew that I could heal myself. Healing is different than curing…

Again, I did the 3Fs process. Again, I faced the judgments and the fear. Again, I experienced the sweet power of forgiving and releasing. The bitter taste of betrayal disappeared from my mouth. I felt so much better. I was able to walk, to eat, to enjoy my life. I expressed gratitude to my body for the messages, and I expressed gratitude to God for guiding me through my own forgiveness process. I expressed gratitude to myself for the courage to see beyond the symptoms and really listen to what my body had to say.

I eventually started feeling a sense of peace and freedom, and from that place decided to speak with the people who replaced me with another speaker at the last minute. I decided to speak up for myself! Something had changed inside of me, and I was able to change my pattern of just "swallowing" my pain and humiliation.

Our bodies are our sacred containers, and we sometimes don't treat them like we really love them. I did see a doctor at one point to assuage my husband's worry, and when she was examining me, she touched my lower abdomen and felt the inflammation. She asked me what I'd eaten, and I told her that I'd had a yogurt.

She exclaimed, "Wow, your poor stomach is trying so hard." When I heard those words, I felt emotions coming up. I was "trying so hard." I have been trying so hard to keep up with everything in my life, and as a result, I had been swallowing so much pain over the years.

Later, I reassured my stomach that it was not a "poor" stomach. (How often we get upset at our "bum" leg or "lazy" eye or "disgusting fat" tummy!) I expressed my love and gratitude for myself. I asked God for help. I wanted to allow healing to occur by letting go of the idea that I had to try harder to make things happen, to keep up with life, to be loved, even to forgive. Miracles occur when we open ourselves and allow the light to come through the "cracks."

I'm not saying that you should not go to the doctor or take medicines; be conscious and do what you should according to the circumstance. But do ask your body what messages it is trying to convey to you. Sometimes doing just that will solve and heal your own "dis-ease," and you might also find a spontaneous "cure."

## I Hate My Shoulder!

At the end of one of our sessions, Tracy exclaimed, "I hate my shoulder!" I asked what that was about. "I'm sick and tired of dealing with this excruciating pain – it's like being frozen." I suggested that we explore the emotional and psychological implications of her shoulder pain in our next session, but she made a face and said, "It's just physical" and left.

It is my belief that no pain in our bodies is "just physical." To discover the true source of our pain, we need to be open and willing to dig deeper. When we can't quite see where our pain really comes from, we need to search for it in our minds and hearts. We need willingness to see and hear the hidden messages.

I suspected that Tracy would want to learn more about her pain, but she had to go through some resistance first. She didn't want to be held responsible or be "blamed" for the pain she was experiencing. She needed to understand that her unconscious patterns were the ones running the show.

Tracy said she had been working with a chiropractor as well as her personal trainer at the gym. She had even had x-rays taken of her shoulder. The more avenues she tried, the more frustrated and upset she became. Nothing worked, and her x-rays only showed minor deterioration, nothing that would account for the extreme pain she'd been feeling for the past year and a half.

At first, Tracy didn't want to acknowledge that her physical pain – the sensation of being "frozen" – was the physical expression or manifestation of an emotional issue. Eventually, she was able to see the truth and said, "I always knew that this was emotional, but I didn't want to admit it. I thought, 'How could I hurt myself? I couldn't be that stupid!'"

We worked with the emotional energy of her shoulder, and as we progressed, her issues surfaced. Even though she'd done forgiveness work around the issue, she was still angry with her husband for the intimate relationship he'd had with another woman. Tracy was having trouble letting go of that pain.

She explained that though everything was now fine with her husband, thoughts of his betrayal kept returning to torment her. She felt "frozen" by her inability to experience joy, and her negative attitude was reflecting that. But she didn't want to express it, so her shoulder was expressing it for her!

As we worked through Tracy's pain, we discovered at a deeper level that it was about her need to open her heart, so she could fully experience and transform the betrayal, the hurt and deep grief of feeling that she wasn't enough for her husband. She had always thought her husband completed her, and when he turned to another woman, she felt lost. Even though they eventually were able to overcome the emotional distance his behavior had caused, Tracy hadn't let go of the judgments she held against him and herself.

When Tracy finally stopped resisting and fully embraced her deep sorrow – her "frozen" feelings – she asked me, "So what do I do now, Clara? I don't want to be frozen anymore! The pain is almost unbearable!"

I responded with, "Forgiveness, forgiveness, and yes… more forgiveness."

It is important to be kind to ourselves as we work with healing our addictive patterns. In Tracy's case, her "addiction" showed up as a frozen shoulder which "covered" her feelings of anger at being betrayed. As we work with these patterns to uncover our true feelings, we chip away at their power over us, and little by little, our addiction – to a person, substance or behavior – diminishes. The effects are cumulative; the more we do our healing work, the more we experience joy, inner peace and love in our lives.

When we feel any negative emotion, such as Tracy's deep-seated mistrust of her husband, that feeling is caused by our judgments.

Here's what actually takes place inside of us:

- Something happens/I do something.
- I decide if what happened, or the action I took, is "good" or "bad" based on my beliefs. In other words, I make a judgment as to whether it's good or bad.
- If I judge the event or behavior as "good," then I feel good. If I judge it as "bad," I feel bad.

If we dwell on those concepts, we come to realize that *we* are responsible for our feelings. We create them; no one else can take the credit or blame for the way we feel. The key here is to realize that *we* are making judgments that cause our negative emotions. Our thoughts dictate our emotions, so when our thoughts reflect the judgments we hold, we experience emotions that are in sync with our judgments.

Our healing occurs when we release the judgments. One of the most effective ways of doing this is by forgiving the judgments we've made – that is, we need to forgive ourselves. True healing begins when we release these judgments and choose a path of love and learning. When we forgive our judgments, we open ourselves to Divine Grace. Forgiving our judgments is crucial for the healing work, and going through the whole 3Fs process, as outlined in Chapter Two, is pivotal for "detoxing" our emotions and thoughts.

## Healing Addiction

The late Dr. Gerald G. May, pioneer in blending psychiatry and spirituality, defined addiction as "…any compulsive, habitual behavior that limits… freedom… All of us," he added, "suffer from addiction." Think of the thing, behavior, person, that limits your freedom. Maybe it is your phone, which creates the illusion of connection, but in reality disconnects you from the people you are with. Maybe it's the piece of cake or anything that you feel you have to have.

When we think of addictions, we think of those substances that seize us physically – alcohol, cigarettes, drugs and food. In recent years, we've heard more about behaviors that grip us as fiercely as those substances, including gambling, exercise and sex. But we can be addicted to more subtle, insidious behaviors and attitudes. Gossiping is a good example – don't you know someone who can't seem to carry on a conversation without spreading some rumor or criticism?

Anger, codependency, control, isolation, jealousy and perfectionism can develop into addictions. Power has been proven to be addictive when it grows to be the primary focus of our lives, eclipsing everything else (as all addictions do). Sports, gaming, politics, actually anything that controls us, including something as seemingly innocuous as playing chess, which looks harmless until it becomes an obsession, otherwise known as an addiction.

The reality is that those behaviors are NOT limiting our freedom… we are doing that to ourselves. We are using them to mask something else. My perspective is that we are limiting our own freedom by engaging in an addiction, which means we are the only ones who can recover our freedom. The first step is taking responsibility. It is not your significant other, the alcohol, or the casino that is to blame. When we are able and willing to take responsibility for our own shortcomings, for our own shadow, we are able to uncover the reason behind the addiction.

It is only then that we can have our freedom back. No matter what form our addiction takes, we need to realize that it sprouted and mushroomed for one reason: our own negative judgments of ourselves. Healing will happen when we are able to release our judgments and forgive ourselves for the behaviors underlying our judgments.

Addictions bring up shame, and most people will do anything to hide the shame that, in turn, only causes more addictive behavior. In this case, the addiction becomes more limiting since most people judge themselves for the addiction and the shame they feel. We need to be willing to see behind the addiction and commit to taking action in the direction we want to go. We also need to be willing to ask for Divine assistance. That is when true healing begins – when we forgive our judgments and shame, and proactively choose the path of love and learning. When we forgive ourselves, we open to Divine Grace.

*"I do not claim love cures everything,*
*but it can heal and in the process, cures occur also."*
—Bernie Siegel – *Love, Medicine and Miracles*

## Healing and Curing – Knowing the Difference

It's vital to realize the distinction between healing and curing. A cure is usually seen when an imbalance, or dis-ease, responds to a treatment and can be measured as an objective outcome or resolution. Healing, on the other hand, is something broader that only the patient can really appreciate. Joseph's story (raped as a young boy and suffered from a mysterious illness as an adult) is a good example of what I mean by "healing." In his 60s, Joseph was diagnosed with a rare "virus" that was killing his body and literally had him by the throat. Part of Joseph's illness affected his ability to speak.

His voice was muted, it turned out, as a result of his efforts to stifle the truth of his terrible experience in an attempt to protect himself. Self-protection of this nature (also known as denial) can help a person live through trauma, at least initially, but ultimately, the "self-protection" will cease to serve the person's higher need to heal. In a strange way, what once helped him feel protected was what was killing him.

Joseph's problem is a perfect example of the way in which old hurts can become "stuck" and turn into health issues, including cancer. As a society, we have acknowledged the relationship between stress, anxiety and heart disease, but any number of health issues can result from holding on to resentments and anger.

My goal is to help you recognize that some of your physical symptoms might very well be caused by old resentments, and that the 3Fs can not only relieve symptoms, but in some cases contribute to the healing of very serious "dis-eases" such as cancer.

As Joseph opened up to the truth of what had happened to him when he was a young boy, he began to be able to use his voice again. His mysterious symptoms began to disappear, and he was eventually completely "cured" – his lab tests came back in the normal range. The more he opened up and spoke about his traumatic experience, the more pain, resentment and shame he released. What he had kept hidden for so long came up to the surface of his consciousness and provided him with the opportunity to heal on many different levels in his life.

*"If you let go a little, you will have a little peace;*
*if you let go a lot, you will have a lot of peace. If you let go*
*completely, you will discover complete peace."*
—Achaan Chah

Even when a person is sincerely doing inner work to heal their physical issue, they may not experience a complete cure. That person may still have to deal with the "outer consequences" of their disease. But because healing is a whole-body-mind-spirit experience, profound healing can happen even when a cure hasn't yet occurred.

I have worked with cancer patients looking for holistic counseling and life coaching, who were able to heal conflicts and imbalances within themselves and their relationships, but still died from the cancer. The difference was that those people were in a place of deep peace, instead of fear and resentment, at the time of their deaths. The "healing" process is about so much more than survival on the physical level. It's about living in the present, joyfully embracing the moment, experiencing gratitude, and dying with acceptance and grace.

Author Eugene O'Kelly, in his touching and inspirational memoir, *Chasing Daylight: How My Forthcoming Death Changed My Life,* vividly described the journey of awakening and transformation he experienced after being diagnosed with brain cancer. He wrote the book in the three-and-a-half months between his diagnosis and his death in September, 2005.

His haunting, yet extraordinarily hopeful message reminds us to embrace the fragile, fleeting moments of our lives – the brief time we have with our families, our friends and even ourselves. This is a clear example of someone who experienced healing but not a cure. Ultimately, we want to experience both, but the path to awakening opens when we use our disease to experience healing. The question is, how do we do this?

To attain change and therefore, transformation and healing, we need to increase our awareness and be willing to dive into the unconscious. We need to let go of our patterns, judgments and misbeliefs, so we can forgive everyone and everything, opening our hearts and minds to other possibilities. Do these practices give us certainty that we will be cured? Absolutely not – but we certainly will be healed, and with healing, cure is closer than we think.

This is a beautiful note I received from the daughter of a client who died from cancer recently: "With an incredible heavy heart, I want to let you know that my mom passed away last night. Even though she declined very rapidly, it was clear that she was more and more at peace. She said before she passed that she was blessed to have a healed and open heart. My father, who had been distant from her for years, was by her side at the end. We are grateful that you led us on this journey of forgiveness. Thank you."

## Forgiveness Makes Us Healthier!

I have found hundreds of clinical studies that establish clear connections between forgiveness and dis-ease or other physical maladies:

- A study by Johns Hopkins Medicine called, "Forgiveness: Your Health Depends on It," established that anger causes changes in our heart rate, blood pressure and immune response (that is, how your immune system recognizes and defends itself against bacteria, viruses and toxins). Those conditions heighten the risk of depression, heart disease, diabetes and other conditions. Therefore, forgiveness calms stress levels and brings better health.

- A 2012 review conducted at Luther College in Decorah, Iowa discovered that in adults aged 66 and older, even conditional forgiveness of others is associated with a [lower] risk for all-cause mortality. In other words, those who learn to forgive can live longer.

- Another Luther College study conducted two years later found the same connections in young adults; they suggest that a "more forgiving lifestyle" may "help minimize stress-related disorders."

- The opposite is also true: Researchers in a 2014 study published in the journal *Psychological Health* found that *not* forgiving can block wellness: "Unforgiveness may have its association with self-reported physical health through its interruption of other positive traits that typically confer health benefits."

- The relationship between forgiveness and physical pain is also well established: A 2005 study published in the *Journal of Pain* examined 61 patients with lower back pain. It showed that those with higher scores on forgiveness-related measurements reported lower levels of pain, anger and psychological distress.

- Getting good rest counts: Subjects in a 2005 study in the *Journal of Behavioral Medicine* showed that sleep quality has a positive connection to forgiveness and less association with a desire for revenge.

- A study at the University of Wisconsin-Madison was one of many that related forgiveness to heart health: "Forgiveness intervention," the researchers wrote, "may be an effective means of reducing anger-induced myocardial ischemia in patients with coronary artery disease."

- Another study found that forgiveness "may play a role in the health and life satisfaction of people with traumatic SCI (spinal cord injuries), with the benefit depending on the type of forgiveness offered."

- A 2012 study from The Spears Research Institute in New York City found that, after talking with 1,629 participants, religious *feelings* (not pressure) were related to greater forgiveness, which led to reduced hostility. This was related to better "subjective health." The message in their study, we believe, is that forgiveness is a process. Like everything else in life, it usually doesn't operate in a vacuum.

Below are a selection of powerful quotes from a few more university-based researchers about the efficacy of forgiveness in healing physical and mental health issues:

- "Chronic unforgiveness causes stress. Every time people think of their transgressor, their body responds. Decreasing your unforgiveness cuts down your health risk. Now, if you can forgive, that can actually strengthen your immune system." —*Virginia Commonwealth University*

- "Unforgiveness is classified in medical books as a disease… refusing to forgive makes people sick and keeps them that way. With that in mind, forgiveness therapy is now being used to help treat diseases, such as cancer." —*CBN.com paraphrasing comments from Dr. Steven Standiford, chief of surgery at the Cancer Treatment Centers of America*

- "Of all cancer patients, 61 percent have forgiveness issues, and of those, more than half are severe." *—CBN.com paraphrasing comments from Dr. Michael Barry, pastor and author of the book,* The Forgiveness Project.

- "Forgiveness could boost the immune system by reducing the production of the stress hormone cortisol." *—Rockefeller University, New York*

- "The program's preliminary work suggests that forgiveness lowered the stress hormone cortisol that in turn affects the immune system, but only when the patients forgave the ones they blamed." *—University of Maryland-Institute of Human Virology*

- "When you hold onto bitterness for years, it stops you from living your life fully. As it turns out, it wears out your immune system and hurts your heart." *—Stanford University Center for Research in Disease Prevention*

- "Those who received forgiveness training showed improvements in the blood flow to their hearts." *—University of Wisconsin*

- Researchers at *The Ohio State University* found that the highly stressed women they studied had lower levels of natural "killer cells" than women who reported less stress. "Natural killer cells have an extremely important function with regard to cancer because they're capable of detecting and killing cancer cells. Psychological interventions, such as forgiveness, have important roles in reduction of stress and improving quality of life but also in extending survival."

- "Fifty-seven well-documented cases of terminal cancers showed the same pattern: the patients chose to release their anger, resentment and depression, and their cancer was gone. They were considered miracles." —*Yale Medical School – Bernie Siegel*

Holding on to anger, hate and resentment – living in a state of chronic unforgiveness – can, according to medical research, lead to cancer. Chronic stress depletes important adrenaline reserves and breaks the all-important oxygen "Krebs cycle," a series of eight chemical reactions that make up the metabolic pathway in all organisms. When that cycle is interrupted, the door is open to cancer mutation of our cells.

One of the main causes of cancer is emotional toxicity. We have all experienced the "toxic" energy of a negative person. I'm sure we can all recall encounters with people whose very presence made us feel sick or nauseated, freaked out or alarmed, depressed or angry.

Emotional toxicity is negative emotional energy – anger, fear, shame, guilt, depression, bitterness, jealousy, envy, hatred, resentment – that has not been processed, released or transformed. If our toxic emotions can "infect" people who are near us, just imagine what kind of havoc they're wreaking on us!

In general, people have been conditioned to believe that treatments for cancer must always be harsh, drastic and violent. But there is hope: Clinicians have found that forgiveness, used as a therapeutic tool along with appropriate medical treatments and lifestyle changes, is a "first-line" primary treatment for cancers. With our "war on cancer" mindset, it's hard to imagine that something as gentle as forgiveness could be the answer to such a serious problem.

*"Forgiveness '…has nothing whatsoever to do with other people. Forgiveness has everything to do with the person giving forgiveness. It is a decision that we make for ourselves.'"*
*—Foundation for Well-Being*

## Forgiveness Can Get You Through the Most Difficult Times

In 2008, journalist Amanda Lindhout was kidnapped by extremists in Somalia and held for 15 months. She was only released when ransom was finally paid. In 2014, the *Educational Journal of Psychotraumatology* published a discussion with Amanda and Katherine Porterfield, PhD. In that piece, the journalist talked about forgiveness and how it helped her survive:

"No matter how many times I was abused, I always felt the same things – disgust, hate, anger, rage – thick and powerful, like a poison inside my body, causing me physical pain. I knew at the deepest part of myself that feeling hate so deeply was not healthy. The rage I felt scared me; it felt alive inside of me. When my abuser would leave the room, I would choose a mantra to say over and over, with controlled breathing, to calm down. I'd learned this, somewhere, years before. My mantras were often, 'I choose freedom,' 'I choose peace,' and 'I choose forgiveness.' I would say this over and over, for an hour, until my body felt calm. I was learning the power of the positive mind… I had a clear vision in my head of the healthy woman I wanted to become again… Forgiveness was an active voice but not an easy one."

Therapists now use these techniques to help survivors of trauma, so they are able to become stronger, regain their physical and emotional health, and rebuild their lives.

*"The winds of grace blow all the time.
All we need to do is set our sails."*
—Sri Ramakrishna Paramahamsa

## Forgiving to Heal Cancer

I met Zue at a cancer expo in Irvine, California. I was giving a talk about forgiveness and how forgiveness can help cancer patients during their healing journeys. I shared with the audience some of the experiences I'd had with various clients. Almost all of them had said they felt "resentment," and acknowledged that holding grudges didn't help them feel any better.

Zue stayed after my presentation to talk with me. Her question was, "So did I get cancer because I didn't forgive?"

"Of course not," I reassured her. "It's not that unforgiveness causes cancer. It's that the suppression of anger, resentment and grief disrupts the normal operation of our bodies. These disruptions lead to weakened immune system responses, and it's this weakened immune system that opens the doors to illnesses and diseases."

Zue then explained that she carried the cancer gene, so she felt there was nothing she could do about her health. She felt helpless and defeated by the disease.

I am not denying that you may get cancer regardless of your emotional well-being. The genetic link to cancer has been well proven, and some people who *don't* carry the cancer gene, who are emotionally healthy, may undergo some other immune system breakdown that *still* allows cancer to grow. But it is also true that the connection between repressing your feelings and contracting cancer is one of the well-documented links in medical research.

I shared with Zue some conclusions made by cancer researchers:

- Stanford University researchers found that women who repressed their emotions were more likely to show disruptions in the normal balance of the stress hormone cortisol. (This can cause alterations in immune system response and suppression of the digestive and reproductive systems.)
- *The Journal of Psychosomatic Research* reported that extreme suppression of anger was the most commonly identified characteristic among 160 breast cancer patients.
- A University of Colorado study found that people who repressed their emotions after a traumatic event had lower immune systems than those who shared their feelings.

Several months after we'd met at the cancer expo, Zue called to schedule an appointment with me. When she arrived at my office, she mentioned that even though she was taking her medications and her condition was improving – and doctors were optimistic about her future – she still felt "really weakened inside" and wanted to try other options.

Zue was feeling drained and knew that the "leaks" in her energy were caused not only by the chemotherapy treatments and the stress of what she was going through, but by the unresolved issues inside of her as well. She said she harbored a lot of resentment toward her mother; she never felt really loved by her and had not been able to let go of that hurt. The more Zue thought about it, the more her anger grew.

We worked together for a full year. I supported and encouraged her to release her feelings of "not being loved." Through the process of releasing, forgiving and letting go, Zue was able to develop a new relationship with her mother, and with herself. Forgiving her mother and forgiving herself for the judgments she had brought to the situation allowed her to grow in a positive way. She started feeling energized, even during the most difficult periods during of treatment.

She began to be able to accept her mother and feel more compassion for her. The mirror effect of this process was that she also began to accept herself and her own life. Without feeling pressure or guilt, and with eagerness for what her future might hold, Zue allowed her mother into her life again. We used the 3Fs process to help Zue transform her resentment into positive feelings that led her a complete recovery.

Zue experienced healing *and* a cure – her cancer is in remission! She still needs regular checkups, and to take care of herself, but she now approaches her health and well-being with an open heart and mind. Whenever she finds herself "in grudge mode," as she puts it, she calls my office and schedules a session. "I need to stay in forgiveness shape," she explains. "I want to stay healthy inside and out."

*"The world can only change from within."*
—Eckhart Tolle

## The Teacher is Often the Student

I have had more than one opportunity to practice my own coaching and forgiveness techniques. Back in 2009, I was diagnosed with a skin condition in my vaginal area that could have ended in cancer. It was extremely painful; I was told it was an autoimmune disorder. I followed that diagnosis with several biopsies to monitor my condition. I had to be checked every three months; the skin was very delicate, and almost any movement caused discomfort and pain. I felt sad and "limited" by my illness.

My dermatologist, who also was a Zen master, told me that the body sends messages. I decided that I wasn't going to experience what a lot of people with that condition had undergone – cortisone, frequent biopsies and even skin transplants. So I did what I counsel my clients to do – I used my inner work process to dig deep and listen to the messages my body was sending me. What was the story behind this condition? What was I suppressing on the emotional level that was creating this painful physical condition? What was my body trying to tell me that I was not hearing?

Memories of events that occurred during my childhood surfaced, and I remembered that I'd escaped from a man who'd tried to molest me. The memory didn't evoke pain. The only emotion that was present was a feeling of being proud of myself for being courageous and strong. Nonetheless, I opened my heart to release any known or unknown judgments that I might have been holding related to that event. Sometimes we don't need to know what happened to experience the bliss of letting go. Judging ourselves for not knowing doesn't help and can keep us stuck in the process. Sometimes, it even creates more shame.

I then looked at my present life and began to understand why my body had chosen to communicate with me in this way. I listened, I treated those parts with kindness and love, and I let go of the idea that whatever was happening to me was unfair. I did the whole forgiveness process, not once, but thousands of times, until no judgments were left inside of me.

My doctor was amazed at my progress. The pain was diminishing, and my skin was getting stronger. I no longer had to undergo biopsies every three months. I used every technique I knew – visualization, loving care, and, yes, a lot of forgiveness. I believed that I was being healed. I didn't know if I was going to be cured, but I certainly was being healed!

Almost seven years have passed. I am healed and almost cured of a dis-ease that doesn't have any cure. It wasn't easy to let go of so many judgments – guilt, ideas about sex, other notions that got in my way – but I did the work, and I was healed.

It seems that because I've chosen to be a healer – of hearts, minds, bodies and souls – I'm often in the position to learn about what I practice on a very personal level. In other words, I continue to learn how to be a better healer by dealing with messages from my own body that sometimes come in the form of illness and "dis-ease." Even though I do the inner work, clearing judgments, going through forgiveness processes regularly, meditating and praying, I find myself dealing with physical challenges specifically so that I can experience first-hand the effectiveness of the theories I teach and believe in.

In 2014, I was diagnosed with loss of bone in my jaw. I was about to travel to Europe when my endodontists – I went to three different ones – all suggested that I have my back tooth removed and get a dental implant right away. I didn't feel comfortable taking such a big step in a rush, so I decided to wait and do more inner work. I went ahead with my travel plans and carried antibiotics and strong pain killers with me in case I needed them.

To support my inner work, I got a picture of what that part of my jaw would look like if I could strip away the tissue and see the bone directly. I also read about bone growth in that area and started visualizing the bone growing back. At the same time, I gave my jaw bone a voice and worked with Compassionate Self-Forgiveness to identify and transform any misinterpretations I had about those bones. I also sent Loving Light to the bone. A year later, I had a healthier jaw bone, my gum was almost back at its normal level, and I didn't need the "emergency" surgeries that were recommended by three specialists.

I'm not suggesting that you ignore your doctor's advice, but this work is preventive and also helps when your body gives you the message that something is wrong. It is important not just to hear it, but to carefully listen. I really encourage you to do the inner work and take the actions you consider to be the best for you.

## Healing with Forgiveness

The path to healing involves forgiveness, and "healing by forgiving" begins with honest answers to these questions:

- What is the story you tell yourself about why you are not as healthy as you'd like to be?
- Are there things you'd like to do in your life, but you complain that you can't do them? What are those things?
- How is it "benefiting" you to keep complaining and turning away from what you really want?
- What would it take to change the situation?
- How do you hold yourself back from making those changes?
- What judgments have you made about this (health condition, illness, disease)?
- Are you willing to let go of those judgments?
- If yes, are you willing to do the forgiveness work that will lead to letting go of your judgments?
- If no, why not? What good are those judgments doing you?

- What actions are you willing to take in order to experience healing, and perhaps cure?

After you've answered these questions, there are a number of techniques you can practice to support your transformation and stay more connected to your higher self in the process.

## Mindfulness

A decade ago, relatively few people understood mindfulness, but it has since gone mainstream. Even hospitals incorporate it into their treatments; patients participating in the Duke Integrative Medicine Program at Duke University, for example, are introduced to the body-mind relationship and the concept of mindfulness. "Mindfulness is at the core of everything we do," says Jeffrey Brantley, founder of the program. "We believe that the more mindful people can be as they face health challenges, the healthier they will be."

The way I practice mindfulness is by being aware of my thoughts, my emotions and my actions. I say to myself, "Now I'm thinking this…" and "Now I'm feeling that…" I do this without feeling the need to do anything about my thoughts or feelings. I simply become aware. My thoughts are just that, thoughts; I don't have to act on them unless I choose to.

Buddha says about mindfulness: "This is the direct path for the purification of beings, for the surmounting of sorrow and lamentation, for the disappearance of pain and grief, for the attainment of the true way, for the realization of nibbana (non-attachment, or the extinction of lust, hatred and ignorance), namely the four foundations of mindfulness." He taught that it is the direct path to liberation.

## Earthing

Earthing allows you to turn to Mother Earth to connect with yourself and the Universe as a whole. Being in touch with water, nature and trees helps us to transform. I personally love the profound healing I experience near the ocean or among the Giant Sequoias.

You can choose your own place of healing, but you don't need to travel to an exotic place to experience nature. Clinton Ober counsels in his book, *Earthing: The Most Important Health Discovery Ever,* "Sit, stand, or walk on grass, sand, concrete, plain dirt – preferably wet… for greater conduction of the Earth's electrons. These are all conductive surfaces from which your body can draw the Earth's electrons. Wood, asphalt, glass and vinyl are not conductive."

Do this for 30 minutes a day as part of your daily routine.

## Music

Play it, sing it, dance to it or just listen. The healing power of music is well documented and is used in hospitals and nursing homes. I particularly enjoy listening to the healing sounds of Tibetan bowls. It is always a deeply spiritual experience for me. I sense the vibration in my entire body.

## Transforming Breakdowns into Breakthroughs

Sometimes, we want to simply escape, to eradicate the experience we are going through! But what if, instead of fighting the experience, we find the beauty within us as we live through the challenges in our lives? And what if, after we find that beauty, we use it to "transform" in the same way that a butterfly emerges from a chrysalis? We can become the alchemists of our own lives, and create new, better, more fulfilling lives instead of fighting for "recovery."

In the Shamanic traditions of ancient times, suffering was treated as a tool for transformation. Breakdowns – physical or emotional – were seen as signs that a form of rebirth was under way. The sufferer retreated to the forests, and if he or she survived the ordeal, he or she returned a transformed person. These individuals were then considered Shamans, the ones who could use their experience and wisdom to assist others.

How can we in modern times use this as a metaphor? How do we retreat to our own inner forest and emerge as "Shamans"? All of you who are looking for an alternate path through a challenging illness or "dis-ease" have the opportunity to use the forgiveness process – your own "inner forest" – to release and transform the toxic emotional energy that is "speaking" to you through your physical illness. Your illness is not a curse, even though you may feel like it is sometimes. Through forgiveness, your illness can become your path to greater self-acceptance, self-love and self-realization.

✦ ✦ ✦

# CHAPTER SEVEN

# UPSETS, JUDGMENTS AND LIMITING BELIEFS

*"The real voyage of discovery consists not in seeking new landscapes, but in having new eyes."*
—Marcel Proust

E very time I drive into Los Angeles, I pass the airport where there is a huge wall with a mural advertising a certain beer. As I'm crawling along in the infamously congested Los Angeles traffic, that ad draws my attention. It is wildly colorful and huge, but ironically, it's the ad slogan that actually catches and holds my attention: "Live life unfiltered..." *Wow! How would it be to live life unfiltered? Without the filters of our own making? Without our own self-imposed limitations?*

Most of us experience our lives through filters, or glasses with different colored lenses according to what we want to or are conditioned to perceive. When we see life through the filter of tinted lenses, we are not seeing clearly. Of course, not everyone gets affected the same way by the same circumstances. We all have our own colored glasses. To experience life without filters, we have to be willing to take off our "glasses" or at least clean the lenses! If we are conscious of our filters, or lenses, we are capable of becoming aware of the behaviors and patterns that alter our perceptions, which then allows us to let go of our preconceived assumptions.

Most of us first put these glasses on as children and replace the lenses as we grow older, as our perceptions shift and change. We hold on to our beliefs and judgments (our filters or "glasses") because we feel they protect us as we navigate our lives. The truth is that we experience upsets because we see "reality" through our glasses or our pre-conceived notions. When we believe something has happened "to" us, we interpret the incident according to the glasses we are wearing. We then create stories about what happened, attach meaning to those stories, and form judgments, which require us to update our glasses.

Just imagine a simple situation: Your partner – husband/wife/boyfriend/girlfriend – calls at the last minute and says he/she has to cancel a dinner date with you because of a late meeting at the office. Your mind can go crazy and make a lot of assumptions if your lenses are colored by doubt and distrust because of past experiences. You feel upset immediately because you start creating stories like: he/she doesn't love me enough, I'm not important, he/she is having an affair, he/she is betraying me... You can go on and on and on. When you clear or remove the lenses, you may still feel those fearful feelings, but you know you are making assumptions according to past hurts that were (but are no longer) the defining stories of your life.

When you take the glasses off, you let go of the pattern of assuming that you are not loved, not important and a victim of betrayal. You are able to accept the situation for what it is. You might not like it, but you don't react to the situation based on old patterns or assumptions; you simply respond in the moment. Upsets are emotional reactions to anything that disturbs our outer and, therefore, inner peace. Upsets often cause us to judge the disturbance (person or situation) as right or wrong, which then informs our beliefs about ourselves and all of life.

Our minds can trick us into perceiving false realities that are actually a reflection of our judgments and assumptions. These experiences influence our emotions and eventually form our limiting beliefs, or they become the different colored lenses we look through. Then these limiting beliefs create our new life experiences, which become patterns we repeat over and over again. These patterns often make us feel stuck in lives we don't want but feel we are powerless to change. It's time to remove the glasses and see yourself and all of life clearly. It's time to set yourself free!

> *"...for there is nothing is either good or bad,*
> *but thinking makes it so."*
> —William Shakespeare's Hamlet

## The Oculus Pit Fall

My son, Seba, had the opportunity to experience the "future of virtual reality" at the 2015 Tribeca Film Festival. I am including the description of his experience because it is an extraordinary example of how our minds can fool us:

*I could see that I was standing in an empty room on flat solid ground. A woman put a device over my head, completely covering my eyes; then she put noise-cancelling headphones on me. A person stood behind me just in case I felt like I might fall. The device* over my eyes turned out to be special set of virtual reality glasses through which I now saw the ground in front of me become a very thin piece of metal with fathomless drop-offs on either side.

I had to walk across this very skinny piece of metal to get to the other side of the room… It was like tight rope walking. It looked and felt as if I would fall into a bottomless pit if I accidentally stepped off the skinny metal path.

I was 100% aware that I was on flat ground and that what I was "seeing" was simply the virtual reality. Nonetheless, I felt pretty scared and was walking very, very, very slowly. My heart was pumping hard, and I felt that if I accidentally took a wrong step and fell into the pit, I would die for sure. But I continued to walk… and walk… I felt like I barely made it across because it was so scary.

When I reached the end, just for fun, my friend who was watching me do this and filming me said, "Step off, Seba." The woman who was running Oculus virtual reality experiment, chimed in, "Yeah, go ahead. Go ahead and step off! Jump off the metal into the abyss!"

I said, "No way, I'm not doing it!" I knew they were standing right next to me and that I was on flat ground but there was no chance that I was going to "jump."

No matter how sure I was that the ground was flat and that I was standing in a room with people around me, my brain was telling me not to jump because I was going to fall into a deep pit and die. But they insisted. So, I went ahead and did it… but I didn't jump. I just barely took a step forward off the skinny metal rail and felt fear deep in my stomach. I literally thought I had fallen into a pit!

*I took off the headset and saw that I was perfectly safe, as I'd known all along. But my heart was pounding and my adrenaline was pumping as if I had risked my life. I couldn't stop marveling at the fact that I knew I was safe but my brain refused to believe the truth and was absolutely sure I would fall to my death.*

As Seba experienced, even when you know without a doubt that you are safe to step off the path you are on and go in a different direction, you may feel too terrified to take the chance. Remember, you should not necessarily believe everything you think you know. Verify the accuracy of your perceptions first.

## Relinquishing Fear and Transforming Limiting Patterns

How many times in your life have you experienced a moment when you knew the truth but were afraid to act for fear that something bad (something created by your mind) would happen? If you feel stuck and unhappy in your current situation, there are examples in this chapter to help you identify the underlying beliefs that are holding you back, and tools to help you transform those beliefs and forgive the judgments that have contributed to the reality you are currently living.

I use examples from my own life as well as the lives of Joseph, Johnny, Tracy and Helena in the exploration and explication of how upsets, judgments and limiting beliefs show up and inform our perceptions of ourselves and our "realities." Due to our life experiences, we each formed a belief about ourselves that made us feel stuck in the realities we'd created!

The facts were real – Joseph was the victim of a sexual assault as a child, Johnny was the victim and perpetrator of violence and abuse, Tracy was betrayed, Helena was a holocaust survivor, and I thought I had to do more to be loved. The families and socioeconomic environments we grew up in, the early difficulties we encountered, and the traumas we experienced made each of us believe something about ourselves and our lives that in time created behaviors, patterns and addictions that were detrimental to our well-being.

The facts of our lives are real, but the misperceptions of reality we each carried came from believing something about who we were on an essential level, due to what had happened to us. In other words, our beliefs about ourselves and our lives were based on events and what each of us made up as a result of those events, NOT on who we truly were and are.

By identifying and acknowledging your conscious and unconscious judgments, thoughts, feelings, beliefs and values, you will be able to see more clearly the false reality you have created and continue to perpetuate. Reality is subjective, and you have the power to perceive your life through the "filter" that supports your truest desires.

Through awareness and forgiveness, you learn to release and transform the beliefs that no longer serve you and create a life that reflects intentional conscious choices rather than conditioned reactions and judgments. When we consciously use all of our experiences to grow and evolve, we make life easier for ourselves and others. As someone I admire said, "The only way to grow is to grow." It sounds simplistic, but it is the truth.

We can "defend" our choice of glasses, or even deny that we have glasses, which are some of the ways we try to protect ourselves from being "wrong," but if we let go of the need to be right and are open to learning, to consciously becoming aware, we will automatically grow and evolve. By being willing to clean or remove our glasses (or even change the color of the lenses), we definitely make our experiences in life more enjoyable.

## Fight-or-Flight Response

One of the ways in which our brains are "tricked" into having a physical and/or emotional reaction to an event is through the "fight-or-flight" response. We are "biologically programmed" for survival. Part of our brain is always scanning for threats. When a threat is perceived – whether real or not – our "fight-or-flight" system is automatically activated. This system prepares our body to respond in whatever way is necessary to defend our lives (i.e., by fighting with a predator or running away).

Our "Survival Brain" is engineered to either perceive a potential new threat or remember a threat from the past and propel us to act accordingly. Even if this perception is false, our fight-or-flight system will be activated. As it happens, a false alarm is quite common in our modern times, since we are rarely in a position to defend ourselves against "predators" anymore.

When our fight-or-flight system is activated, our Survival Brain bypasses our Thinking Brain. Our brains are designed this way so that we can act quickly, without stopping to think, in order to survive. Although the fight-or-flight reaction is automatic, we CAN learn to become aware of the activation and engage our Thinking Brain to make better choices – provided we aren't actually in a life or death situation.

Even though we may feel we have no control over this biological programming, we are still able to take responsibility for our actions and reactions.

*"Between stimulus and response there is a space.
In that space is our power to choose our response. In our
response lies our growth and our freedom."*
—Viktor E. Frankl

## Reaction vs. Choice

There are three steps to managing our reactions and negative emotions:

1. Manage the fight-or-flight reaction while it's happening.
   a. Become aware that you either feel angry (frustrated/resentful/irritated) or afraid (shut down/withdrawn/panicked). Take the time you need to recognize that your fight-or-flight system has been activated as a result of perceiving some kind of danger.
   b. If it's a real-and-present physical danger, take care of yourself first, non-violently if possible.
   c. Set an intention to calm down, and take the time to respond wisely.
   d. Pause and breathe, as this helps rebalance your nervous system so that you can respond, rather than react.
2. Clear the effects of a fight-or-flight reaction in your body, and release or transform any corresponding emotional responses. Emotions are just that, energy in motion. It's important to take the time to observe the energy and consciously tune into the fact that you don't need to act on your feelings. Take a short walk, and use your breath to consciously release the energy.
3. Learn from the reaction. What triggered the reaction/fight-or-flight system, and was it an appropriate reaction? Look for

situations in which you were similarly triggered. What other choices did you have?

## The Roles We Play Create Our Reality

The fight-or-flight response is biologically programmed to ensure our survival in the wild, just as our beliefs and values are programmed by our families and cultural institutions to ensure our survival in society. The "roles" we play in our families become the first "filters" through which we begin to create our future reality. These "roles" determine our sense of self, inform our judgments and form our beliefs and values. Each family member has an unspoken identity: the smart one, the pretty one, the self-sacrificing one, the emotional one, the hard-working one, the troubled one, the sensitive one, the irresponsible one, the demanding one, the charmed one, etc...

Our families play a role as whole, and value one specific role more than others. Members of the family unconsciously play the game... who sacrifices the most, who is the most successful, the funniest, and so forth. We all play the game until we become aware of it; we play to gain love, recognition and appreciation, even if it is through pain and sacrifice.

We all interpret the rules of the family game in ways that prevent us from seeing clearly, we are seeing through the perceptions and projections of our families, peers, educational institutions, cultural values, religious beliefs, political positions and the circumstances of our own lives.

Often, the values and practices we absorb are supportive and help us become strong, self-determined and successful. But sometimes the roles we get stuck in follow us throughout our lives and never allow us to become who we really are or live the lives we truly desire. What game does your family play? What game have you been playing your whole life? What is your "role," and does it suit you, or is it limiting you from becoming more?

## Tracy's Role

When I began working with Tracy to help her forgive her judgments against her husband for betraying her with another woman, we found that the blocks preventing her from living the life she imagined for herself went much deeper and had their origin in her early family life. As we moved more deeply into her issues, we discovered that she kept postponing a vacation she needed and deserved because she had too many other people to take care of. She just simply couldn't make the space in her life for herself!

When I asked her why she didn't want to go on vacation, she protested and said that she did, but that she wouldn't be able to truly enjoy herself knowing there were so many other things she should be doing instead. We dug deeper into her family dynamic, and I deduced that the role she had played in her family while growing up (and still did) was the "self-sacrificing one." As she spoke, I could hear from her stories that she was the one who suffered the most, who worked the hardest, who gave the most but never took anything from anyone else in return. I understood that, in this way, she felt valued and could be sure that she would also be the one who was "loved" the most.

I asked Tracy, point-blank, "What role do you think you were playing in your family game?"

Tracy replied with hurt in her voice, "What game? I didn't play a role! I don't play games!!"

I then asked, "How does your persona as the self-sacrificing saint impact your present life with your husband and kids?"

Tracy was visibly shocked that I had called her out and answered defensively, "What are you talking about?!"

After a while she became aware that she was so attached to her role that she couldn't see it. After thoroughly investigating the dynamic, she conceded that her self-sacrificing pattern of behavior was not only having a negative impact on her life and freedom, but was compromising her relationship with her husband and children. By refusing to take a vacation, she was denying family fun time and limiting their experiences.

The "benefit" she received from this behavior was that everyone felt sorry for her and made exclamations about what a good person she was because she always put the needs of others before her own. This may have worked within the context of the family she grew up in, but it was damaging her relationship with her husband and the family she was raising.

Tracy's breakthrough was powerfully emotional. When she could really "see" the reasons behind the reasons for her present problems, she was shaken to her core. She finally understood how she rationalized everything. She acknowledged that she had created "good" excuses to protect herself, so she could be the "winner" of the game. So she could be the one who was valued and loved for her sacrifice.

Until she took the mask off, uncovered her eyes and was willing to see it for what it was, she was not able to experience the huge relief of being herself and of living her life fully. She was shaking and crying as she saw her entire life, from the beginning until the present moment, unfolding in front of her like a fast-motion movie showing her how she was never able to fully experience pleasure.

Tracy announced, "I'm done with this! I'm willing to work on this, and really, I mean really, let it go!" I was so proud of her willingness to face herself without judgment and move forward from a position of awareness and determination to change. To completely let it go, she needed to be willing to cooperate. She was now ready.

If you feel stalled in your current life and unable to break out of patterns that don't serve your intentions, by identifying the game your family played and understanding the role you had in that game, you can begin to uncover and transform the limiting beliefs and values that have contributed to your "misinterpretation of reality."

By "misinterpretation of reality," I mean the version of life you are living that conforms to unexamined, often unconscious, judgments and values you took on through automatic (flight-or-flight) responses and cultural/societal programming. When your "programming" is still running the show, you are seeing, and thus experiencing, life through the filters that were put in place a long time ago. In order to change your life, you must clean, or better yet, replace, the old filters with updated ones that reflect the new beliefs and values that support the life you want.

## Victim Consciousness

Johnny's story provides a powerful example of a profound "misinterpretation of reality." Johnny was not an empowered person though he tried to act as if he were. After working with him, it became evident to me that he was making choices from a disempowered point of view. Because he was blind to his disempowered self-concept, he often felt victimized, especially during his younger years, and blamed others for "forcing" him to make decisions he didn't want to make.

At a conscious level, he didn't consider himself to be a victim, but everything he was doing in his life was from a victim position. The truth is that he had the power to make his own choices, but because he unconsciously perceived himself to be a victim, he felt that against his will, other people always made choices for him. He believed for a time that his girlfriend's behavior "forced" him to take action against her; he didn't want to kill her, but he felt he had no other choice.

He felt powerless, though he would not have characterized himself as a powerless person. He simply perceived the world to be full of bullies, when this was actually not the truth. This was something he was able to acknowledge later, after he had gained some awareness of how his trauma had influenced his perceptions of himself and life in general.

Through our process together, he became aware that the reason he repressed his feelings was because they were so extremely painful. Johnny was victimized as a child, but because he never processed those feelings and then internalized the conclusions he made, he attracted experiences over and over again in his life in which he felt victimized. The misperception of reality for Johnny was that he was a "Victim." He constantly encountered situations in which he felt he was being pushed or even forced to do things he did not want to do.

Though he was victimized once, he unconsciously adopted the position – the limiting belief – that he would be a victim always, which made him feel deeply unworthy and disempowered. When we are victimized we feel like victims and we perceive that others are attacking us even when that is not true. The problem is, when we define ourselves, unconsciously or not, as the victim, it can become a self-fulfilling prophecy in that the unreal threats we perceive can eventually become real threats and situations in which we are again actually victimized. You will see it if you look for it…

Joseph also held the belief that because he was victimized he was always a victim; he held that at an unconscious level. Before he spoke to me, he had not revealed the episode in his childhood that had caused him to internalize the victim position. He had not spoken to anyone about this incident for 50 years, not even his wife. When we believe something, we act according to that belief, so if we believe we are victims, we make decisions from that belief. We sit in the victim seat and run our lives from there. Changing the belief allows us to experience life differently.

## Healing the Memories

I use a process with my clients that is called "Healing the Memories." In that process, we go back in time to the traumatic event in which they were victimized. In Johnny's case, it was not easy to get back to the memory of his molestation at the hands of his stepfather. He was an innocent child when it happened, and at the time, he locked the painful event inside himself. It took us quite some time to unearth the decisions he'd made about himself in that moment.

While it is true that many of us are victimized at one point or another during the course of our lives, in order to heal from those experiences, we need to discover the decision we made about ourselves in that moment. When we do that, we are on the path to healing and, therefore, the path to awakening.

When we lock our pain inside ourselves, we lock God out and experience separation, hurt and pain. When we let the misunderstandings and misperceptions go, we expand our consciousness, we open the doors to liberation, we let God in. Then we experience integration, not separation.

Through our work together, Johnny was finally able to let go of his identity as a victim and take dominion over his life. When we become aware that we are holding a limiting belief, we are able to work through the underlying emotional issues and release, transform or reframe the belief.

Sometimes, when we undergo a particularly painful trauma, it can be difficult to unearth the limiting belief we formed about the event, ourselves or life itself. In this kind of situation, it is important to seek the help of a professional who can lead you gently through processes that will help you see the truth and give you the opportunity to heal in a safe environment.

## Feelings and Upsets

Some of our feelings come from our beliefs and judgments. When we judge something as "good," we feel good when it happens. When we judge something as "bad," we feel upset/angry/sad when it happens. These emotional reactions become habits so that the same feelings are triggered over and over again, even when the circumstances are different. Most people don't realize that it's often our pre-programmed beliefs and judgments that cause us to feel upset. This upset causes us to lose power to those beliefs.

If we want to empower ourselves, we need to ask ourselves: What do I believe about this situation? What are the judgments I'm making about this? Answering these questions honestly frees us from the limiting beliefs that are causing us to suffer. We can then "update" our software, and we can switch out the pain code for the empowering or transformation code. When we do this, we are on the path to our own inner liberation and, in a way, our own enlightenment.

Freedom comes from being true to ourselves by transforming the "fake" or pseudo-self that has been covered up by irrational beliefs. We empower ourselves by becoming aware of and updating the old beliefs we took on while growing up, and letting go of judgments and knee-jerk reactions. Then we are free to choose beliefs that really work for us.

Our projections onto others, our judgments of them and ourselves, and the beliefs we hold in our minds limit our life experiences. When we identify our inner judgments, we begin to free ourselves from a host of burdens, because our judgments of others are actually judgments of ourselves. They are defensive emotions that we believe keep us safe. But what these judgments actually do is give us an excuse to feel superior or inferior and separate from others, rather than connected and compassionate.

Some of our feelings are reactions to thoughts and experiences. These feelings can determine the kind of thoughts, judgments and beliefs we form. In time, our emotionally charged thoughts, judgments and beliefs are reflected in our bodies. Understanding that some of the tension we hold in our bodies is a reflection of our negative or limiting thoughts, judgments and beliefs gives us the means to lessen their often debilitating effects. We cannot always control what happens in life, but we can control how we react to what happens.

It is possible to learn to consciously use our breath to release negative or limiting emotions we hold in our bodies so that we have a greater ability to choose how we react and what we think. When we are conscious about where anxiety and other negative feelings reside in our bodies, we are empowered to start the liberation process. We can consciously direct our breath to those parts and release what could otherwise get "stuck" at a cellular level. Our breath becomes a valuable tool for relaxing our bodies and, in time, changing our minds.

## Limiting Beliefs

One of the more hurtful and persistent limiting beliefs I have held against myself is the belief that "nothing I do is ever enough." Over time, that belief expanded its reach and became: "I am not enough." As an adult, I became aware that this belief was running certain aspects of my life, especially after I had an upsetting confrontation with my mother.

Becoming *aware* of the irrational beliefs that hold us back and destroy our self-esteem is one of the first steps to breaking free of self-imposed limitations and an overall misinterpretation of reality. There are ways to consciously uncover the limiting beliefs that are running our lives, but it is often an uncomfortable encounter or situation that brings forward the realization that we are reacting in accordance with a belief that may not be serving our best interests.

The day I had the emotional confrontation with my mother, I was helping her in the hospital where she was recovering from broken ribs as a result of a fall. She accused me of not taking care of something or other… I remember flushing with righteous indignation and humiliation. I was doing sooo much! Her lack of appreciation struck me like a punch in the gut, and I remember almost doubling over. My eyes were brimming with tears I couldn't control. *Why did she always have to hurt me? Why did I give her the power to hurt me like this?*

I blurted out, "Nothing I do is ever enough!"

I had done everything I thought she wanted me to do, and no matter what, it was not enough to make her happy. I was very upset, but felt guilty at the same time. I hadn't done anything wrong and I felt guilty anyway. I felt I had to apologize for crying, for having my feelings, for not doing enough… even though it was not true and I knew it!

While I was driving back home from the hospital, the phrase I'd blurted out in the hospital popped up in my mind again: "Nothing I do is ever enough." For the first time, I saw how that belief was being played out in the other areas of my life. I knew that it wasn't about her, and the part of me that felt guilty wanted to run back and apologize for my feelings. At a deeper level, I really *knew* that she was doing the best that she could, and this was bringing to the surface my own unresolved issues.

I had begun crying so hard that I had to stop my car and pull over. As I cried, I thought, *even if I'm a good and loving person, I don't receive the love I want to receive or I don't receive it the way I want to receive it. Even though I work so hard, I don't have enough money to cover everything I need… and now I'm taking care of my parents. I don't have enough time to relax… I don't have enough time to enjoy anything.* One after the other, all of the places in my life where I didn't have enough, or where I felt I wasn't enough came into my mind. I thought, *I don't have enough. At the end of the day, it's never enough.*

I didn't have *enough* in my life. I could never do enough, and I would never be enough. That's what I perceived and, as a result, that's what was showing up. My life was reflecting back to me situations in which I perceived that there wasn't enough (time, money, love) or that I wasn't enough – good enough, smart enough, energetic enough, loveable enough, etc.

When I understood that I was "creating" my reality by perceiving myself and my life through the filter of such a limited point-of-view, I really GOT it… *This is not my mother's fault. She can say or do whatever she wants, but it's not true that I am not doing enough. I am doing more than enough. And it's not me. I am enough.* When that awareness came to me, I experienced my heart as fully open. The only feeling I had was pure love. I felt deep compassion for my mother and for myself.

I had unconsciously defined myself as someone who always had to do more, be better, study more, achieve more and give more. It never occurred to me that the other side of the coin was: I have to do more because I am never enough. Sometimes, our beliefs and misunderstandings are hidden in this way. We need to be willing to open our eyes and flip the coin to see what we find. I did finally realize that unless I released those perceptions and limiting beliefs, nothing would ever be enough, including me.

Releasing the misperception that I wasn't enough meant that I had to accept that I was in fact enough and that I was doing my best and so was my mother. In order to effectively transform the limiting beliefs that I was not enough and that nothing would ever be enough, I also had to release the judgment I had against my mother for wanting me to do more and more, as well as the judgments I had about her being unfair, and about life being unfair. In a sense I was being unfair to myself.

How did I do that? With Forgiveness! Forgiving the judgments underlying the misperceptions and the limiting beliefs is essential to the process of transformation.

*"Life is very simple. We create our experiences by our thinking and feeling patterns. What we believe about ourselves and about life becomes true for us."*
—Louise Hay

## Freedom from Limiting Beliefs Exercise

1. Find a place where you feel comfortable and at peace.

2. Turn off the TV, phones and any other distracting device.

3. Light a candle and put on soft, soothing music. This will send a signal to your senses that it's your time for yourself.

4. Take a deep breath and become present to yourself.

5. Give yourself permission to explore and to look inside.

6. Think of something that upset you recently.

7. Ask yourself, "What happened? How did I feel? What did I do?"

8. Allow yourself enough time to explore the details.

9. Ask yourself, "What did I make of this? What did I judge? What are my beliefs about what happened?" (Tip: Every time you find yourself saying should, it means there is a judgment.)

10. Give yourself permission to look to this situation from a different perspective. How would this look from the heart, not the hurt?

11. Using this perspective, how would you feel different?

12. Can you bring compassion to yourself and the situation? For example, you feel betrayed by someone you love and you judge them, but if you unearth a situation in which you betrayed someone else, it will help you understand that you

sometimes fall short of your own expectations. Understanding paves the path to acceptance and ultimately compassion. You don't have to like what happened, and sometimes parting ways or making different choices will help alleviate the hurt. But compassion and forgiveness will heal your heart and soul.

Regarding the situation you just used for the exercise, ask yourself: "What conclusions have I made about myself that limit me?" For example: "I don't deserve good things in my life." Or, "Nothing good ever happens to me." This is another version of feeling like a victim. There are also: "I'm stupid, a failure, etc…"

Ask yourself what kinds of choices someone who held those beliefs about him/herself would make. Give yourself time to explore your feelings and conclusions. For example, if someone feels ashamed, they might be reluctant to take responsibility and might blame others or try to hide the truth.

So, once you are aware and willing to let go of the judgments associated with those beliefs, and see the truth (the truth is that you made those choices or judgments according to the level of consciousness you had), you can create a different life for yourself. But first, you need to hold different thoughts. If you update your belief system, what kinds of thoughts would you choose to believe about yourself? How would you show up in life if you had these new thoughts?

# Dark Secrets

One way to discover or uncover a limiting belief and/or a total misinterpretation of reality is to recognize and acknowledge our dark secrets. These are the secrets we not only keep from others, but the ones we try to keep from ourselves. I say "try," because the truth is that no matter how much we try to push shameful feelings out of sight, they are always with us, and we have access to the root cause of those feelings if we choose.

I do admit that it takes a certain amount of courage to face shameful, painful feelings, but the ultimate benefits far outweigh the temporary reprieve of denial. The upsets, judgments and limiting beliefs that hide behind our dark secrets are the keys to our freedom. When we face our shameful secrets, we have the power to transform the limiting beliefs that are keeping us from being all that we can be.

When we hide something, most of the time, it's because we are ashamed of it; we don't want others to find out. Joseph kept the abuse he suffered hidden; it was his "dark" secret. He used his vital mental, emotional and physical energy to hold and protect the secret inside of himself. By doing so, he was killing himself from the inside. The emotional pain that was not released and the suffering he experienced that was not processed for 50 years took a toll on him.

Because of what happened to him as a child, the innocent boy made a lot of "assumptions" about who he was: He was an object of shame, he didn't deserve to be happy, and he was powerless. Of course, he didn't know at that time that those assumptions would become the limiting beliefs that would almost kill him later in life.

Until he became so ill that he had to confront his past and reframe the limiting beliefs that came from the assumptions he made about himself after the rape, Joseph believed he had "forgotten" what had happened to him. By "forgetting" the actual attack, but unconsciously retaining the limiting ideas he formed about who he was, he kept the attack alive inside of himself.

Some part of him felt that the only way he could go on, the only way he could survive was to protect himself from the suffering the attack caused by sublimating his real feelings. He tried to keep it a secret from himself and felt that if others didn't find out, they wouldn't judge him. It would be like it never existed. So he kept it secret out of shame. He made an agreement with himself that he would never talk about the attack, and in that way he closed his heart.

While getting my master's degree in Spiritual Psychology, I learned a lot about dark secrets and the effect they have on our lives. In one of our classes, we learned how to create a genogram, which is basically a family tree that traces the invisible patterns and secrets carried from one generation to the next. The book *Family Secrets: The Path from Shame to Healing* by John Bradshaw clarifies the different categories of dark secrets and how we can carry the patterns for generations without even knowing it.

When I first constructed my genogram, I didn't know that there was someone missing in my family tree – the son my husband had fathered with another woman. I have since reconstructed the genogram to include this formerly "secret" member of our family. I realized that I didn't want to "transfer" that hidden pain pattern to the next generations in our family. I wanted a message of love to be handed down to my son and the ones to come after him. I wanted forgiveness, acceptance and love, not revenge and hatred. When we forgive, we not only free ourselves from the burden of the pain we have been carrying, we have the opportunity to heal the generations to come.

Creating a genogram can help us understand how dark secrets limit our life experience and freedom. When we are able to understand and accept the mistakes and weakness of our own family, we can then free ourselves from the patterns that have been passed down from generation to generation. The energy we use to keep those secrets can drain us, make us ill and sometimes even kill us.

## From Fear to Freedom

Our minds tend to focus on the negative, and the more we focus on our negative thoughts, the more we have the tendency to go into "catastrophe" mode. Sometimes we have genuine issues and problems, but the issue that scares us the most is often irrational and all-consuming. We fix our minds on all the things that can go wrong, we try to control our emotions, but in reality our mind is the cause of our reactions and responses.

What do we do when we experience fear? We try to control the circumstances; we are alert to anything that could "mean" that the thing we fear the most is going to destroy our lives. Can we really control them? People, circumstances, situations? Not really. We believe that we can by being alert and vigilant, which is good in certain life or death situations, but not in our daily lives.

Just a couple of years ago I was living in "catastrophe" mode, even though I was not showing it. I was going through a challenging time in my marriage at the same time that I had a lot of other stresses in my life including money problems and difficulty finding the time to write my book. Persistent thoughts about my husband and the state of our marriage plagued me: *Why is he (my husband) behaving strangely? Why doesn't he love me (the way I want to be loved)? Why is he so unstable? We already went through so much… why this now?*

His instability was reflecting back to me the fears of instability I was experiencing. I was supporting clients going through similar issues and counseling prisoners dealing with their demons, but I just couldn't get over my own pain. I kept asking myself why I was focusing on this part of my life. It didn't make sense because there were also several other areas of my life that were not going the way I would have preferred. So… why the focus on my marriage?

I used the Forgiveness Process, but it wasn't until I worked on my fears that I could start my own "Freedom" phase. My fear was that I was going to lose my husband… but it was more than that. I kept asking myself what the fear was really about. My pain and fear continued, the forgiveness continued, but I wasn't experiencing relief.

Was the problem that I was not really forgiving all of my underlying judgments? Or was there something hidden in my unconscious that was still playing a big role in the story of my pain? Interestingly, a shift in my obsessive worrying about my marriage occurred when my husband and I had some financial issues we had to take care of. But after those financial issues were resolved, my mind went right back to obsessing about the state of my marriage.

In a sense, my happiness depended on his happiness, even though I coach and counsel people on this. *I do happiness coaching for God's sake!* I told myself. *And I'm attached to his happiness??? What else do I need to learn?* I was laughing at myself! Believe me, laughing at yourself is truly healing! I knew the answer to my question at a mental level, but I needed to know it at a heart level. My healing eventually came about because my intuition was telling me that it was more than that, and I was willing to listen to my intuition.

My deepest fear was losing my family… When I truly connected with this fear, it shook my whole body. I saw myself as a little child praying in the school chapel for my parents. Something inside of me was scared to death that I would lose them. Over time, because I could not quell that fear, I learned to live with it.

The fear was like a roommate that was sometimes quiet, and sometimes loud and clamorous. Sometimes I thought it had moved out, but then it would show up when I least expected it. I learned to live and play with it when I was a child, but that fear had been dormant for years until I began worrying incessantly about losing my husband. The fear was in control of my inner life. I felt it in my throat and my chest.

What was the attachment? If I could find the attachment, I could find the judgment. The attachment was to my family, to the idea that without my husband I wouldn't exist. I had to detach myself, my identification with my marriage, and accept the hurt, the pain and uncertainty that we are sometimes confronted with in life. I had to be willing to let that go. That was the only way to forgive the judgments that were keeping my heart prisoner. That was the only way to experience inner freedom and, therefore, inner peace. I knew I deserved it. We all do.

## Process for Healing and Transforming Perceptions of Limitation

In order to heal and move on from my painful preoccupation, I focused on going through the process I developed for my clients and offer in my book *Soul Journey to Freedom*:

Tip: Observe your words. Your words show where your focus is. If you want to release or transform your judgments, fears and misconceptions, observe your thoughts and words!

1. **Revelation:** I had the awareness that not only was I afraid to lose the relationship I had with my husband, but I was afraid of losing what "family" meant to me. I believed that my family was everything, and without my family I was nothing. I believed I was not being a good mother/woman/wife if I was not able to keep us together NO MATTER what. I had

to do anything and everything to keep my family together; otherwise I was nothing. My identity would be wiped out. Although I knew this wasn't true on a conscious level, until I became aware of the root cause of my extreme fear, I wasn't able to know what was truly operating inside of me. That fear was separating me from Love.

2. **Acceptance:** Acceptance is such an important part of this whole process. We need to accept the hurt, accept our human-ness. Sometimes we try to "cover up" the real reason (if the reason doesn't exist, the fear is not real). Instead of healing so that we may reside in the peace that is always present inside of us, we "give energy" to that fear. It is by embracing that part of ourselves with love and compassion that we start the integration process. Have you noticed that when you don't want to think about something, it's exactly what you think about the most? The same thing happens when we try to "convert" those parts of ourselves we consider to be unac-ceptable. It is by accepting and loving them that we can let them go. They might be around, but they don't have energy any more. We don't "kill" them; we love them.

3. **Releasing, Forgiving and Transforming:** We can be our own alchemists. We don't kick those parts out that we don't like; we forgive ourselves, others and the situation. We do this by releasing the energy and by forgiving the judgments. We can then transform those negative thoughts into healthier thoughts that are more in alignment with the kind of life we want to create.

4. **Envisioning:** It is so important that we "see" ourselves being who we want to be and living the way we want to live. Seeing

ourselves as we want to be provides us with an opportunity to use our imagination. In my case, I saw myself as I am: a dancing, singing spirit, empowered in my inner love, strong, trusting that everything is okay. Affirming is the process of sending our brain and our bodies the message we really want. My affirmation is: "I am loved, held and protected by God! All is good in my world!" This is the process that also helps us reframe what happened to us. Sometimes by going through difficult times we learn about patience and kindness, and we develop more understanding and compassion. We can reframe what happened into something positive. Of course, it can be difficult to find the positive, so even if a reframe is not applicable, learning about compassion and forgiveness can open miraculous doors inside of us.

*"NOW is another name for God, NOW is another name for Heaven, NOW is another name for joy, NOW is where you get to leave your ego behind and meet your whole Self."*
—Robert Holden

✦ ✦ ✦

# CHAPTER EIGHT

# MOVING ON FROM HURT

*"To make a deep mental path, we must think over and over
the kind of thoughts we wish to dominate our lives."*
—Henry David Thoreau

## Living a Heart-Centered Life

How can we reframe our painful experiences to empower ourselves and move on with our lives? Moving on means giving ourselves permission to remember our heartfelt dreams and turn them into reality. How do we make the conscious choice to relate to others from the heart rather than the hurt?

A heart-centered life is lived from a place of authentic empowerment, empathy, compassion, understanding and love, never from a position of self-judgment, martyrdom, resentment or hatred. You might be wondering how to live a heart-centered life if you feel broken-hearted.

To live a heart centered-life, the first thing you must consider relinquishing is the notion that your heart is broken. Once you begin to understand that your heart is always whole, and that the broken feeling is actually the result of the barriers you have constructed around your heart in reaction to pain, you are on the path to reconnecting with your heart energy and opening to a "heart-centered" life.

*"You can only be held back by your past if you use it to reject yourself in the present."*
—Robert Holden

## Healing Is In the Present

Over 20 years ago, my husband, our then very young son Seba, and I went on vacation to Switzerland. One beautiful day, while taking a break from sightseeing, we sat on a park bench next to each other for a brief rest. Seba was sitting in the middle, wedged between me and my husband. I loved the warmth of his small hand in mine. I was daydreaming, remembering the day he was born, completely absorbed in my thoughts, basking in the sunlight on that lovely summer day. All of a sudden, Seba pulled his hand free and pinched my arm.

Startled, I looked at him and said, "Hey! That hurt! Why did you pinch me?"

He laughed with the innocence of a child, and said, "Mom mami ya paso! Asi es la vida." ("Mom, it's over! This is how life works.")

I asked, "What do you mean?"

Still laughing, he replied, "Mom, everything is like this! I'm going to pinch your arm again." He did just that and said, "It hurts, but it's over now. So you just have the memory... but you have to think about that, Mom, because it is NOT happening now!"

I said, "What if I have a bruise on my arm now?"

He sighed deeply and said, "Mom… it is just a bruise that makes you remember… but it is over."

This concept applies to the healing and forgiveness work we are doing here. Healing occurs in the present. When you go back to the painful memories of the past and stay there, you get stuck in that moment, you live life from that perspective. When you're stuck in the painful past, you experience your present life through the scrim of past memories, living with the fear that those hurtful events might happen again, or with the false expectation that one day the pain associated with the memories will magically disappear.

If you want to create a different future, you need to do it from the present moment. And to be truly present, you must have healed the painful past. This healthy present is a place where you no longer feel the need to press on the bruise just to recall the old pain. From this place, you have the choice to create a different future.

This doesn't mean that what happened to cause your pain was not important. It can takes a while for the bruise to disappear or the wound to heal. If we don't want the wound to become "infected," we need to face it. We cannot forgive if we don't allow ourselves to fully experience our pain and grief first. After we have done the work, after the hurt has been faced and processed, we have an opportunity to let go and move on.

After doing all the work I am offering in this book, when you feel ready to move on, allow the past to live in the past. Instead of recreating it, just let it be. Understand that it cannot be changed; accept what happened and be willing to create today the memories of tomorrow. As Seba said, "It is just a bruise." You don't need to keep looking at it. And with time, it will fade away. It is not happening now, unless you continue to reimagine the pinch that created the bruise over and over in your mind.

I do not in any way mean to deny your suffering! Believe me, I wish we could change things that happened in the past – choices, decisions, things we did and said, and things that were done to us – but accepting that we cannot change the past is the first huge step to creating a different future.

## Have I Really Moved On?

How do we make sure that the forgiveness work we have done is complete? What if we find that there are more pieces of resentment left? What if we fall back into our old patterns? Do we have to start the process all over again?

The kinds of thoughts you have about the person or situation you have been working to forgive will give you all the information you need to determine whether or not you have moved on or are still attached to the pain. Do you feel genuine acceptance for the circumstances, yourself, and any others who may have been involved? Or, do you secretly feel ashamed or angry that you have "forgiven," or that you have reconciled – if that is the case?

A powerful clue that you may not yet be ready to move on is when a part of you feels that you shouldn't let go, shouldn't forgive, shouldn't accept the situation and/or the person. Being obsessed with the person who hurt you or fixated on the situation are other clues that you may have work to do before you can move forward. Thinking too much about the motives behind the other person's actions and continuing to doubt their remorse are also signs that you still have unresolved resentment inside of you. Another indication that you are not ready to move on is when you feel disgust, irritation or antipathy every time you are with the person or think of the person who hurt you.

If you find yourself lashing out at that person without any apparent cause, it means that you still need to do more work on resolving your feelings and healing your hurt before you will be able to move forward in the relationship or with your life. Living your life with seemingly unresolvable feelings of resentment (even if they are submerged and "controlled") impairs your capacity to live life joyfully, lovingly and happily.

If you want to move on, you must check inside yourself to see if there are still lingering resentments and/or residual hurts that are preventing you from opening your heart, trusting the other person and yourself, as well as feeling love, joy and pleasure. The 3F's process can be used continuously as a transformational tool to help you work through old and new emotional upheavals. This work never ends. The only way to avoid the forgiveness work is to be free of judgments, and it is difficult to live a life free of judgments 24/7. I don't expect you to be perfect in this regard, but if you live in a place of awareness, you can learn to diminish your judgments.

## Matthew's Journey to Authentic Forgiveness

One of my clients, Matthew, had "forgiven" his fiancée for a liaison she'd had with another man on the night of her bachelorette party. He felt extremely hurt by the incident, and her excuse – "I was sooooo drunk!" – didn't do anything to make him feel better. In spite of this, they loved each other deeply and wanted to repair the relationship, so they decided to postpone the wedding until they were able to work out their feelings.

They came to see me for couples coaching, and after a few months of deep work, which included individual sessions, they decided to move forward with their plans to marry. However, every time a small issue would arise, an argument would inevitably ensue, and the bachelorette night incident would come to the surface again. Ultimately, they ended up arguing about that night over and over again. Matthew's fiancée was ashamed of what she had done, and he felt ashamed that he had actually "forgiven" her.

In spite of these fights, Matthew kept claiming that he was over the whole thing and willing to move on. I believe he genuinely wanted to get married and put the past behind them, but he wasn't able to get past his feelings of hurt, shame, humiliation and resentment. He confessed that when he was with his friends, he kept wondering what they thought of him for still wanting to marry the woman who had cheated on him. He couldn't let go of his resentment. He was not ready to move on.

During our individual sessions, Matthew and I worked on what the cheating incident really, I mean REALLY, meant for him. The primary emotion underneath the other emotions was his feeling of profound unworthiness as a human being. These deep emotions were Matthew's shadow or hidden feelings. Until he faced all of his emotions and worked on transforming his feelings of unworthiness and inferiority, he would not be able to truly commit to moving on with his relationship.

He needed to experience the fullness of his pain in order to heal. He was afraid to go into the dark places in his psyche. I explained that in order to liberate himself, he needed to unearth the old pain and release it before he could honestly face what was happening in his relationship. His thoughts and the conclusions he'd made about past experiences were driving his emotions, which were causing the unrelenting pain.

Matthew finally admitted, "I'm not enough of a man… otherwise she wouldn't have done that."

That thought kept coming back every time they had sex, and it was completely disempowering for him. We used the 3Fs process, and it wasn't until he was able to forgive the judgments against himself (not man enough, rejected, inferior) that he was genuinely able to start the process of healing. When he healed the past, he empowered himself in the present, which allowed him to make a conscious decision about what he truly wanted.

So many times we want to avoid reliving or bringing back those dark moments or memories; we experience fear, we don't want to feel the same feelings again. If we are to experience freedom, we need to move through the fear of revisiting those places with the intention of healing and liberation.

## The Shadow Is a Powerful Teacher

If you have done the 3Fs Process and still occasionally get blind-sided by strong negative feelings (which is also referred to as getting "triggered"), you are likely encountering your shadow. The shadow is the part of you that feels unworthy, insignificant, ashamed and alone. This part does not believe you deserve to be loved or respected. This part hides because it is mortified for feeling so weak and vulnerable. This is the part that can come to the surface even long after you have forgiven a person or a situation that has hurt you. Your shadow is the part of you that hides deep, painful emotions under your surface emotions of anger or indignation.

Having a loving conversation with your shadow instead of fighting and struggling with that part of yourself will help you begin transforming the fears, doubts and insecurities that characterize the shadow. By embracing the shadow, you show yourself compassion and acceptance.

By accepting yourself, "warts and all," you create a safe internal space that will allow healing to come about more easily. By loving your shadow, you can bring about the transformation that will allow you to begin to feel empowered rather than disowned, denied and degraded. You will then be able to turn something that looks like a weakness or a liability into your strength.

Until we are willing to explore our own darkness, we cannot fully heal our pain, hurt, fears and insecurities. We can then shed light on our own darkness by bringing acceptance, love and forgiveness to the disowned or shadow part of ourselves. When we shed our light, our love, onto that part, our shadow fades and eventually disappears.

*"When you hold resentment toward another,*
*you are bound to that person or condition by an emotional*
*link that is stronger than steel. Forgiveness is the only*
*way to dissolve that link and get free."*
—Catherine Ponder

## Releasing Emotions

Even though you have gone through the 3Fs Process and have come to a place of relative equanimity, you may find that painful emotions occasionally come up again in relation to the person or situation that hurt you. These may be unresolved residual emotions having to do directly with the person or situation you have worked to forgive, or they may be deeper, more complex emotions related to your shadow issues. Either way, releasing your emotions through tears, vocalizing (screaming and moaning), physical activity or free-form writing will allow you to energetically let go of the pain you are holding inside your body and soul.

If your feelings arise in a social setting, try counting silently to 90. There is scientific evidence that when you count to 90, the negative feelings diminish enough so that you can begin to think clearly again. This recommendation is meant not only for people who are having an emotional reaction in a place where they actually might harm another person or themselves, but for anyone who wants to avoid reacting by saying or doing things that they might later regret.

After you have counted to 90 and feel the energy of your emotions defusing, observe yourself. This observation is a crucial aspect of the healing process. Observe your energy level, your thoughts and feelings. Observe your reactions and interactions. Ask yourself the question, "What is this bringing up for me?"

Observing yourself when you're in a situation where you felt triggered, is akin to hiking up to the top of a tall mountain in order to observe everything below from a higher perspective. After you have reached this new perspective, if you are still feeling triggered, write a letter to the person who triggered your emotional reaction. DO NOT send the letter! It is for your eyes only. It provides a safe place for you to express your feelings. Don't hold back... Allow all the pain and darkness to surface for clearing. After you have finished writing the letter, do not read it. Bless it and burn it (in the sink or fireplace, or outside in the grill – in other words someplace fireproof).

Often, the revelation of the truth of your pain and the power of your feelings will bring up tears, moaning and/or the desire to scream. If this happens, allow yourself to slow down and cry, moan and/or scream. (If you are concerned that your screaming may scare or alarm others, you can scream into a pillow. Be sure to air out your pillow after you have screamed into it!) Let yourself be vulnerable so you can release and transform your pain, and open your heart to deeper levels of healing.

## Ready to Move On

Often, people feel the desire to be done with the healing process before the healing is complete. That happened to Joseph several times. He believed that when he finally let everything come to the surface and worked through the pain, it was over. He wanted to live a "normal" life. After a long talk between us, he was able to define what living a normal life meant for him. It was feeling free to do the things he liked, being able to give and receive love, being able to laugh and live life fully. It was a life that wasn't "ruled" by the hidden monsters of the past.

In spite of his profound progress and his ability to live a "normal" life, the old demons would occasionally surface. The 8-year-old boy who was afraid, ashamed and disempowered would still sometimes run the show. He had worked through many of his fearful thoughts, beliefs, misconceptions and misunderstandings, but occasionally the old fears and negative patterns would emerge. When that happened, he tended to get upset, resist the feelings, and try to suppress them, as he had done for the past 50 years.

In order to move on, he needed to accept that healing happens in layers. Sometimes we experience readiness, but that doesn't mean that an old feeling won't surface as a result of a trigger. If we suppress the shadow, we give it more energy, and in a way we are "creating" that monster again.

Joseph wanted to move on, but he did not want to continue to deal with the triggers that brought the past pain forward into his present awareness. Months passed while he was a living a "normal" life, until he one day felt again the burden of deep emotional pain. He did not become physically ill this time, but he became emotionally ill. His life was being run by the scared 8-year-old boy.

During subsequent sessions, he learned to embrace all the aspects of himself, the shadow, the fear and the things he kept doing when he was being ruled by those old beliefs. We worked on forgiveness in order to release the new pain, which was really old pain that was surfacing. He also worked on embracing the concept that moving on means being willing to let the past go, as well as being willing to embrace and love the shadow.

I helped him understand that embracing and loving the shadow would allow him to continue to transform the painful patterns as they arose. This process was particularly challenging for him because he hated his shadow and was reluctant to face and embrace it, just as he had resisted facing what had happened to him in his childhood.

He began to understand that his healing was a work in progress, that what happened to him was THEN, and now was now. He had to remind himself that whatever he was experiencing was not happening now; the memory of it was what caused the pain and despair. We all have to practice this if we want to become free. It is important to remember that we forgive the past so we can heal in the present. He came to understand that he could ruin the rest of his life, or he could build a new life and the future he desired. He had to learn to give himself permission to dream and laugh, and he had to convince the little 8-year-old that he could have fun.

It was important for him to learn to love himself, not only for himself, but so that he would be able to love others. He needed to love the 8-year-old boy. I encouraged Joseph to "embrace" his little 8-year-old self and reassure him that he was safe. I also encouraged Joseph to say to his 8-year-old that he was lovable, and that his essence was pure, innocent and intact.

It was very powerful to be in the presence of this 60-year-old man saying out loud, "I love the part of me who feels betrayed, I love the part of me who feels lonely, I love the part of me who feels dirty, I love the part of me who feels scared and ashamed. I love the boy inside of me, I love myself, I accept myself."

As he spoke these beautiful words, I could see him standing taller as the burden he was carrying on his shoulders was slowly dissolving.

## Forgiveness Maintenance

Tracy and her husband, Kevin, had been working through their relationship issues and were doing well. They had their ups and downs, but overall they were happy. That is exactly what they told me on the phone when they called to schedule a "maintenance session."

When they got to my office, Tracy said, "We have been doing forgiveness work; we have been working our process. We really love each other, and we understand now after so much work that shit happens in life, and we can use it to destroy ourselves or to transform ourselves and our relationship. We have discovered that 'shift' and not shit happens when we're willing to face our own issues and let them go…" She paused and then explained, "I know that all sounds good, doesn't it? But we're here because of a silly, stupid thing that happened the other morning."

I listened to them while observing Kevin, who wasn't feeling very comfortable. I asked, "What happened this morning?" Kevin was not in a talkative mood, so Tracy started talking and explaining that they were having a good morning and that she had been waiting for him for a couple of hours while he finished his work. When he was done, Tracy told him she was no longer in the mood to play golf and asked if they could play later in the day.

He replied, "I'm going to practice by myself or find someone else to play with. We don't have to do everything together."

Tracy overreacted and started crying. "We've done everything we were supposed to do, everything you told us… and yet we're still arguing! He doesn't get me! So what do I do now? How does forgiveness help? Now what?"

Kevin was quiet and seemed not to want to participate in the conversation. He looked like he was very far away. I encouraged them to relax, take some deep breaths and tell me more about what was going on, what the upset was really about.

Tracy was very emotional and said, "I'm really sick and tired of this! It's so unfair!"

"What's unfair?" I asked. Tracy told me the story again and added that her crying had precipitated a big argument.

I asked them both, "What did this mean to you?"

Each of them experienced the moment from a different perspective. They were living reality through their own lenses; we all do. But if we are mindful and aware, we can detach from that. Kevin felt that he wasn't free to do what he wanted; Tracy thought that Kevin was being unfair because he had asked her to wait and then wasn't willing to wait for her.

For Tracy, it really wasn't about playing or not playing golf; it was about feeling like she did everything and received nothing in return. What was the truth? We needed to go beyond the facts to observe the feelings. Nothing Tracy could have done would have given Kevin his own freedom; it didn't matter what she said or did, he always felt that he was a "slave" to circumstances beyond his control.

Tracy could have said, "Whatever you want, honey." Or "I want this…" No matter what, Kevin would have felt he couldn't do what he really wanted. He had to unlock his shackles and came out of his own prison. It wasn't about her. It was his own conditioning. Tracy felt that he was being unfair, and that triggered her unresolved issues. As Tracy had already asked, "Now what??"

Forgiveness helps with the daily issues as life brings us opportunities to keep growing and healing. I remember someone telling me that enlightenment does not happen when you crawl inside a cave and meditate non-stop by yourself; enlightenment happens when you come out of the cave, meet people and learn from the challenges that relationships and life present. The issue you face doesn't matter; the answer to "Now what?" is always LOVE.

What does that mean? Even though you could have been doing forgiveness work, shit happens… and if you want to experience shift inside of you and not shit, you need to be willing to keep up with your forgiveness work. For you to experience forgiveness, you need to be willing to exercise the muscles of compassion, release, surrender and acceptance.

*"Let us forgive each other — only then will we live in peace."*
—Leo Tolstoy

# Redemption

As I mentioned in an earlier chapter, I was at a conference during which Patrick Chamusso, who was in prison with Mandela, shared a story with us. He told us that at some point after he was released, he was walking through a small town where he encountered the prison guard who had repeatedly tortured him. At the moment he saw the guard, he experienced such a powerful urge to kill him that Chamusso thought seriously about how he would do it and imagined the entire scenario.

Chamusso thought about how the guard had almost killed him, and how he must now kill the guard. Then, a very different thought came into his head that was equally strong. Even if he killed the guard, he would not be at peace. The guard's death would not give Chamusso back his life. Mandela had taught him about forgiveness. So, instead of threatening the torturer or killing him, Chamusso walked on. The guard was terrified and ran away.

That was the most important step for him in terms of being able to move on with his life. It was the point at which he was able to experience true and complete forgiveness, and eventually compassion. That was the moment that ultimately compelled him to start creating orphanages for kids who were abandoned because their parents were in jail or had been killed. He transformed his energy, and instead of seeking vengeance and living in a state of hatred, he chose to be of service.

Transforming your energy when you have an emotional urge to get revenge, to hurt the person who hurt you, is one of the most profound opportunities forgiveness offers. By observing ourselves when we are desiring revenge, by staying conscious and aware of what the outcome might be, we have the agency to make a different choice.

Just imagine yourself doing it – transforming "the need" to get revenge with the desire to do something good for others. When we do good things for others, we end up doing a good thing for ourselves. What do you want to do for yourself? Instead of giving strength to the shadow, give strength to your Soul, to the part of yourself that is willing to move on. Let your Soul embrace your shadow with compassion and love, but make your choice to move on.

It's not a requirement, but for certain people, part of the healing process comes through being of service or helping other people transform their pain and suffering. Can you imagine a world where we can transform resentment, vengeance or pain into healing and good deeds? I know this vision might be idealistic, but it is doable; the change starts inside of us.

*"And as you wish that others would do to you, do so to them."*
—Luke 6:13

For Johnny, being of service to others became an opportunity for his redemption and is finally what allowed him to fully forgive himself and find the inner freedom to move on with his life. If we dwell on the desire for revenge and continue to cultivate hatred for ourselves or others, we're going to have a life that reflects our anger and hate. So, we need to ask ourselves, "What kind of life do I want? Do I want a toxic life?" If you want something different, you need to do something different.

After we've done the forgiveness work, when difficult emotions arise, perhaps it means that there is another layer of pain that needs to be healed. We need to peel away the layers of pain as they surface. Sometimes extremely painful memories that we have not been ready to face stay buried inside until we have the strength to peel back the layers. It's easier to project our pain onto others than it is to see where the pain lives within.

When we understand at the conscious level that facing the pain doesn't mean living in the pain, but means that we have the opportunity to transform it in order to really free ourselves, we can muster the strength to go through the transformational process. Transforming pain into something lighter means we have created room for inner freedom and peace. We have to keep doing the process to keep moving on. Maintenance means that we always have to do the work.

## Cultivating Resilience

Forgiving strengthens our ability to be resilient. The more we forgive, the stronger that muscle gets. We learn to be observers of our own feelings and our own lives. Because we are fully engaged, connected to our deepest self, unafraid of our shadow, we can go through hurricanes, earthquakes and personal tsunamis, and not only survive, but thrive! We are able to find a purpose in everything.

Being resilient helps you accomplish your calling. At the end of the day, you don't feel the suffering in such a way that it destroys you. Instead, it empowers you. It doesn't mean that you have to go through suffering to be strong, but when you go through those times, you can find the strength inside of yourself. If you do this work and take the time to actually go through this transformation, you will be able to change your life and experience more of what you want. You will have the focus to pursue your purpose, or unveil what was always present.

As human beings, we will probably continue to need to transform our emotions and our feelings until the end of our lives, but by tackling the really tough stuff and the unconscious issues, the shadow and the early childhood traumas, we develop resilience. By practicing this transformative work, we get to the point where we get through our hurts and our injuries much more quickly and much more easily, which frees us up to spend more time doing what we want.

When I go to bed, I review my day and release any judgments I have made. I also express gratitude. After having done the deep forgiveness work, I find that this daily practice keeps me in "forgiveness shape."

Nowadays, everyone speaks about forgiveness, but real forgiveness is a different thing. Real forgiveness is the key to freedom, which opens the door to unconditional love. So what are you going to do with your life now that it is not defined by anger, pain and resentment? Now what? The path to happiness and inner freedom is wide open.

If you could hear your eulogy, what would you like to hear? Who would you like to be? How would you like to go through life? How would you like to be remembered? What kind of mark do you want to leave on this planet and the people who were around you?

This work helps us find and dissolve the illlusory barriers that separate us from the happiness, joy and freedom already inside of us. The choice is yours. Remember that at a soul level, everything is already forgiven. It is our ego that struggles. This work is like a GPS for the ego to reach the soul level. These tools help give directions to our egos, and it's up to us how we implement them and how many detours we take to reach the soul, our true essence, our authentic self.

✦ ✦ ✦

# CHAPTER NINE

# AWAKENING TO
# THE LIFE YOU WANT

*"You create your thoughts, your thoughts create your intentions,*
*and your intentions create your reality."*
—Dr. Wayne W. Dyer

What kind of reality do you truly want to experience? If you want to experience a reality filled with love, peace and abundance, the life you desire is much more within your reach if you are consciously setting intentions that are in alignment with your desires. By freeing your energy from negativity – fear, resentment, anger, doubt, jealousy, hatred – you give yourself the opportunity to create the life of your dreams.

The energy that has long been attached to anger, resentment, and pain can now be used to awaken. Releasing judgments through forgiveness frees up a significant amount of energy that can be used for manifesting positive results. When you let go of feelings, thoughts and judgments that have bothered you for a long time, you cut the chains that have kept you imprisoned in a jail of your own creation. You are no longer attracting what you don't want from a place of pain and hurt; you are creating from a positive place of inner freedom, self-love, hope and compassion.

Even if you have managed to achieve great success in spite of your anger, your ability to feel the joy of that success is significantly limited. Once the destructive energies in your psyche are sent on their merry way, you can create from a productive, fertile field of possibility. With forgiveness, the opportunities to live in joy and service are infinite.

## The Importance of a Spiritual Practice

Can forgiveness be a spiritual path that opens the doors to our own awakening? While participating in Robert Holden's Happiness Project, a foundation dedicated to expanding and promoting happiness worldwide, I asked him about the importance of spiritual practice in the work we do, and he said that spiritual practice is something we need to do every day in order to love ourselves. When we are too busy to start the day with our spiritual practice, we are rejecting ourselves, and will then find as we go out into the world, that the world will reject us as well.

I admire Robert Holden and his work and have read all of his books. It is powerful to listen and learn from someone who has experienced a lot of pain in his own life and has been able to turn those experiences around. Robert's response to my question was so simple and yet so profound; it struck a chord inside me, and I thought that when we don't forgive ourselves and others, we find ourselves living in a world that reflects back the judgments we are holding.

I have a spiritual practice that helps me stay in "spiritual shape." I wake up every morning and meditate first thing. I raise my vibration by listening to inspirational music or podcasts, and I read poetry or spiritual material. I often admire my garden – smelling and touching the flowers and plants, giving thanks for their beauty. I allow my spirit to be touched by the butterflies and hummingbirds who regularly visit. I pray for acceptance, peace, love and joy. When I go for my daily walk, I express gratitude for my life, my health, my family and even my challenges. Yes, my challenges, because they are the forerunners to new growth and pleasures. Every night before going to bed, I release any judgments I may have made during the day.

## The Happiness Circle

In one of the sessions I had with Joseph, I asked him to step into an imaginary circle. I instructed him to imagine that inside the circle, "HAPPINESS" was written in large, red letters.

I said, "Stand in the circle for a few minutes, in silence... Breathe in happiness, breathe out happiness." After a few minutes, I put a few of the things I had with me – books and notebooks – around him while he was standing in the circle. I then said, "Imagine that these books and things are walls, psychological barriers that prevent you from really experiencing happiness... Please describe them."

One by one, he described the mental/emotional/physical barriers he perceived as limitations. While doing this exercise, he noticed that some of his barriers seemed less dense than he had thought they were. He realized that as a result of all the healing work he had already done, many of the barriers he had perceived as limitations in the past were dissolving and that they were in fact illusory.

I had him step into another imaginary circle that had "THE PAST" written inside. As he stood there, he perceived that the barriers and walls were there and that they were solid. When he stepped back into the "HAPPINESS" circle – the present – he recognized that he was willing and able to cut the cord to the past and live fully in the present. As he stood there connecting with the energy of his newfound happiness, he said quietly, "I'm sad sometimes… how do I dissolve that?"

In a very gentle voice I replied, "Dear Joseph, we all have sadness sometimes."

I encouraged him to say, "I HAVE sadness, rather than I AM sad." After repeating the phrase several times, he really caught the difference in the energy.

I said, "You are becoming aware of a happiness so big that it can hold your sadness. You are building a container inside of yourself that is pure contentment and joy. That means that sometimes sadness exists in that container, but it's neither a wall nor a barrier that prevents you from experiencing happiness."

Joseph still remembers that day and the exercise we did, and when he feels sad, he knows it isn't what he is; it's only a feeling he is experiencing. In his mind, he replays the exercise which brings him back to his own center.

## Choosing Happiness

We have navigated the waters of pain and grief to open ourselves up to the possibility of experiencing happiness. That is ultimately the reason we forgive, to free ourselves from the past, so we are able to live authentically, happily and gracefully in the present. When we are willing to see and accept that we have attracted relationships and created circumstances in our lives that have limited our experience of happiness, we are finally ready to take the steps that will set us free. Every day we are empowered to choose what we want to experience through our creative energy. Are we going to feed the lack, the depression, the dissatisfaction, or are we going to feed the happiness?

There is an old Cherokee tale called *The Two Wolves*. It goes like this:

*A Cherokee elder was teaching his grandchildren about life. He said to them, "A fight is going on inside me... it is a terrible fight between two wolves. One wolf represents fear, anger, envy, sorrow, regret, greed, arrogance, hatefulness, and lies. The other stands for joy, peace, love, hope, humbleness, kindness, friendship, generosity, faith, and truth. This same fight is going on inside of you, and inside every other person, too."*

*The children thought about it for a minute. Then one child asked his grandfather, "Which wolf will win?"*

*The Cherokee elder replied... "The one you feed."*

So what part of yourself do you want to feed?

That does not mean covering up our feelings or not grieving when we need to cry; it means taking responsibility for our emotions, working our process, releasing our judgments through forgiveness, and embracing joy! We are human and will always experience sadness, pain and grief, but if we can accept that fact, do what we need to do to move through our pain and then consciously choose to awaken to the glorious possibilities in life that await us, we can spend more time in a state of peace and happiness than in a place of pain and suffering.

What is it that we want for ourselves? It's our choice. It has helped most of my clients understand that they choose their experiences, but sometimes they say to me, "I don't like the options. And in fact, I don't see any options!"

I always reply, "But one of the options is better than the other for you at the moment." If you don't make a decision, your "choice" is made by default, and you stand to experience being a victim over and over again. When you "choose" to remain a victim because you're not making a conscious decision, you are allowing the hurt, the betrayal, the abandonment, the abuse, whatever happened to you, to make the choice for you.

Do you want what happened to you to make the decision for you about how your life is going to be for the rest of your life? Or do you want to make a conscious decision and use those experiences for your growth and evolution? I understand that sometimes it's extremely painful, but the more we resist and struggle, the more painful it is. Choosing is one of the most powerful tools we have for empowering and supporting ourselves as we continue to walk the path to awakening.

In order to make conscious choices that are in support of your awakening to happiness and inner peace, ask yourself, "What would make me happy?" That answer, of course, is different for every person. We usually think happiness is something we pursue. We keep "pursuing it," putting off our peace and our freedom until we reach it. Even the U.S. Constitution declares that we "… are endowed… with certain unalienable Rights, that among these are Life, Liberty and the pursuit of Happiness." But what exactly are we supposed to pursue?

What if happiness is actually inside of us? Viewing happiness from that perspective is a conscious choice. You can decide to stop chasing happiness, stop waiting for events or conditions around you to change, and look at happiness as something you nurture and develop inside of yourself.

## Grace Through Gratitude

Living in grace is living in partnership with God. When we become conscious of the fact that we have the ability to set the intention to experience happiness, we open ourselves to grace. I choose to experience living in grace through gratitude. Nothing is more life-changing than forgiveness and gratitude. Through forgiveness and gratitude, we become grace.

When we open to the light, we open the path for grace to flow. When we experience grace, there is no resistance, no struggle. We surrender to the divine, and it is effortless. As Pope Francis said: "Grace is not knowledge or reason; but rather grace is the light that is in our souls."

## An Angel Appears

My husband and I were in London and decided to go to Paris in the middle of the week. We had a little less than 48 hours to be there because I had a project I was working on in London and couldn't take more time. I was elated at the idea of being able to take a train under the English Channel that would transport us in less than three hours to the magical city of Paris.

We arrived in Paris and left our small suitcase in the lobby of the hotel where we would spend the night. A musician started playing Ravel's *Boléro* as we were waiting to jump on the cable car to Sacré-Coeur. I just love that piece of music… my eyes were full of tears, my heart open. We entered Sacré-Coeur and I lit three candles. One to express my gratitude, another one to ask God to bless me, my family and the world, and the last one to bring this book to completion.

We stopped at a café for a coffee and a croissant. I love the sense of aliveness I experience every time I sit in a café in Paris. I love people-watching – so many different kinds of people – rushing, strolling, laughing, talking… so invigorating! We spent the rest of the hot afternoon walking through the busy streets, taking pictures of every single thing we could to extend the moment.

Evenings are long during the European summer. We were still wandering the streets of Paris at 10:00 p.m., and the sun was still shining. After a late dinner, the full moon had finally risen, and we went to observe the beauty of the Eiffel Tower from the Trocadéro. It was full of people, locals mingling with tourists. The Tower was all lit up with the moon as part of the spectacle. I was in awe.

I was so grateful to be there! On one side of the Trocadéro platform, there were people dancing to Latin music. I invited my husband to dance, and although he was a little hesitant at first, he joined me. I felt I was one with the music, the night, the Tower, the moon. I couldn't have asked for more.

When we finally decided to head back to the hotel, we couldn't find a Metro station that was open. It was past midnight, and one after another, the stations were closing up just as we got to them. I started laughing and singing, "Last Train to London." There were no taxis, so we continued walking. I had bruises on my feet after such a long hot day, but I didn't care. I was enjoying every bit of it!

My husband asked, "Don't your feet hurt?"

I declared with glee, "I'm walking in the streets of a city I love in your company feeling grateful… so who cares? There are people with bruises on their feet because they are fleeing places in this world where they are being persecuted… and I am to complain about my feet?" I blessed them, as the joy I was experiencing was radiating through my entire body!

We finally got a taxi to our hotel. As soon as we got to our room, we fell into the comfy bed and immediately drifted off to sleep. The next day, we stopped at the Louvre, the Grand Palais, the Pont Neuf and the Pont des Arts where people attach padlocks or "love locks" to the railing or the grate on the side of the bridge.

Couples who attach a lock to the bridge swear their commitment to each other and throw the key in the Seine. I had heard that part of Pont des Arts fell down because of the weight of the thousands and thousands of locks. I wanted to see if the lock we'd put there a couple of years ago was still there. It was impossible to find, but it was just a symbol… love is who we are. We stopped for deux glaces – two ice creams – on Boulevard Saint-Michel, and then again witnessed the full moon over the Eiffel Tower.

The next morning, we went back to London after a beautiful 40 hours in Paris. As we were walking off the train in London, I told my husband that a part of me wanted to stay longer, not from a place of "not enough," but from a place of joy and aliveness. My soul and my heart were singing. Suddenly, his face turned grim and he said, "I have to forget about how tired I am if I want to remember the good moments."

After a few minutes of patiently listening to him complain about how exhausted he was, I started crying. I couldn't understand how he could deprive himself of his own happiness. In a way, I was doing the same by attaching my elation and happiness to his behavior. I felt it was unfair for him to ruin our good time. I was judging him.

I wanted to scream, "Life is beautiful, and it's up to us to enjoy every bit of it. Don't you see?" I was fighting for my happiness, so instead of screaming, I said, "You do whatever you want, but I'm grateful. I'm open and want to receive all the blessings. I want to see the beauty in everything."

We had been planning to go to the Royal Academy of Arts in London that night, but because of what my husband had expressed to me, I told him that we didn't need to go. I could see that he regretted making me cry and felt he wanted to do something for me. So we went to the Royal Academy. I decided to be present with myself and in my joy, totally unattached to the outcome.

We were running late, and it was just five minutes from the start of the concert. My husband was walking a little ahead of me, and I saw him stop and talk to a middle-aged man with grey hair and beautiful eyes. I saw my husband pay him, so I called out, "Don't go crazy just to compensate for being grumpy."

When I caught up to them, the man said to me in a Spanish accent I'd never heard before, "You are going to enjoy this. You have good seats, and this is going to be a treat for you." It struck me that he had been speaking English to my husband, but chose to speak to me in Spanish without having any idea that I spoke Spanish! I looked into his eyes and was about to thank him, when all of a sudden he disappeared.

We entered the Royal Academy and kept walking and walking. It turned out that we had first row seats and had paid less than what it cost to sit in the last row. I felt so deeply the truth that when we are willing to receive the blessing and when we are willing to see the little miracles in life, we receive.

## What Does Awakening Look Like?

As we awaken to our lives, as we awaken to our destiny, our purpose, we begin to know what it feels like to live in a state of grace. Forgiveness is the key that opens the door to awareness, but it's an ongoing process, and everyone has their own pace and their own path to awakening.

Johnny's awakening started when he was able to accept that he was in prison and had to take responsibility for making the best of his situation. He started finding happiness inside of himself when he saw that he could serve others and make a change in their lives even inside the harsh environment of the prison.

For Joseph, both being able to recover his health and feel the integration of all the aspects of himself that he had disowned for so long, were what led him to his awakening. It was not an easy or short path, but being able to laugh again and enjoy life were exactly what he wanted.

For me, awakening to the life I wanted became about relating from the heart and not the hurt. Being conscious and aware of this clear intention inside of me serves a greater purpose. I not only give myself permission to live life fully, but I also leave that legacy for my son Seba, who is living proof that love is the answer. When I relate to my husband Sebastian from my open heart, I'm residing in my loving essence, and I experience grace. It brings me tremendous happiness and fills me with light to be in a loving, fulfilling relationship with him.

Another clear example for me of "relating from the heart and not the hurt" was being able to have a loving relationship with my husband's son Guille. Being in touch with him, being open and available to support him as he grows in consciousness, is what my heart truly wants.

He occasionally listens to my radio show and sends me encouraging texts that say things like: "That was great!" or "I like what you said." Being able to have a relationship with him that is based on compassion and understanding is allowing me to live the life I want, fully open to pure acceptance and joy.

Forgiveness gave me the opportunity to remove the veil and see that there is something bigger than myself. When I relate to Guille from this place, I fulfill God's plan. I don't delve into thoughts like: "I would have liked this to be different," because it is what it is, and I accept it.

One of my clients said one day, "I don't know what has happened to me... and I don't know if you see it or not... but at some point after working with you, everything changed. It has been a subtle change, but I realized one day that I can look at myself in the mirror and I don't judge myself in the harsh way I used to. I don't compare myself to others. I take personal responsibility. I've stopped blaming others for my own circumstances... and I don't know how this happened."

One of the things she hadn't been able to do was go for a walk or a run by herself because the abuse she'd suffered as a girl had made her afraid of being alone. Part of her recovery work was to face her fear and take baby steps toward being on her own outside of her house. When she recounted her new feelings to me, she said she realized that the fear was no longer there. Fear was no longer preventing her from being herself.

She wrote to me explaining that she was seeing colors differently, that for the first time she was seeing the color of the sky, the color of the trees. She asked in the email, "Do you really see all the different shades of green in the leaves?" and exclaimed, "They are all so different and so rich!" She felt alive for the first time in a very long time.

That was her experience after a year of work that wasn't about mining her pain, but was about gratitude and cultivating the choice to be happy. We hadn't gone back to the abuse memory; we had been tackling little things that led her to this place of personal transformation. Sometimes the work doesn't have to be hard or painful. As we awaken to who we really are, it isn't always necessary to continue to relive the painful past.

In life we are so used to being prepared for the storm, the earthquake, the bad things that are going to happen. Ask yourself, "How am I preparing myself for the good in life? Am I open to receive the miracles and the blessings? Am I willing to see the angels in life? Am I showing up? Am I being who I really am?"

*"Our deepest fear is not that we are inadequate. Our deepest fear is that we are powerful beyond measure. It is our light, not our darkness that most frightens us. We ask ourselves, 'Who am I to be brilliant, gorgeous, talented, fabulous?' Actually, who are you not to be? You are a child of God. Your playing small does not serve the world. There is nothing enlightened about shrinking so that other people won't feel insecure around you. We are all meant to shine, as children do. We were born to make manifest the glory of God that is within us. It's not just in some of us; it's in everyone. And as we let our own light shine, we unconsciously give other people permission to do the same. As we are liberated from our own fear, our presence automatically liberates others."*

—Marianne Williamson – A Return to Love

## Mission Statement

One of the ways we can support ourselves to be who we really are and live the lives we want to live is to create a framework for our vision for ourselves. The "Mission Statement," rather than limiting us, gives us wings to fly. It allows us to expand and awaken to our authenticity.

When you hear the phrase "mission statement," you probably think of a company or organization. Their mission statements are "official" answers to the age-old questions, "Why are we here? What is our purpose, and what is our reason for existing?" It wasn't until actor Tom Cruise decided to write his personal mission statement in the 1996 movie *Jerry Maguire* that we realized that people can write mission statements for themselves!

Of course, if you saw that movie, you'll remember that Jerry Maguire got it all wrong! His mission statement, written when he was angry and disgusted with his job, rambled on for 25 pages and got him fired. Still, a lot of moviegoers walked out of the theater thinking, "Hmmm, a mission statement… what a great idea! Maybe I'll write one for myself!"

Most people who start a business wouldn't dare launch their companies without a carefully written mission statement. For a company, the mission statement expresses the corporate purpose; it articulates the company's goals and, most importantly, tells us what the organization intends to do in the world.

A personal mission statement fulfills the same need: All of us function better when we give deep thought to our own mission – our relationships, marriages, purpose and values. We assume that we know what drives us and where we are headed, but few of us pull those thoughts together in a formal declaration. And we need that framework for our lives to be clear about what we want and where we want to go.

Don't make the mistake of thinking of your mission statement as a "New Year's resolution." It isn't about an aim you "want" to achieve this year, or something you feel pressured to accomplish. Rather, a mission statement is the basic fabric of your life; within that statement you formulate your heartfelt desires, your ethical and moral values, and your purpose. It is your personal GPS, continuously reminding you of where you want to go and who you want to be as you travel along that journey.

I encourage you to reflect on these questions as you formulate your own mission statement:

1. Who do you want to be?
2. What do you want people to think of when they hear your name?
3. What do you stand for?
4. What do you offer your relationships – not just your life partner, but friends, parents, coworkers, siblings, children and others?
5. What makes your heart sing?
6. What are your deepest values?
7. What does "success" mean to you?

*"In order to write a personal mission statement, we must begin at the very center of our Circle of Influence, that center comprised of our most basic paradigms, the lens through which we see the world. It is here that we deal with our vision and our values... Whatever is at the center of our life will be the*

*source of our security, guidance, wisdom, and power."*
—Stephen Covey – *Seven Habits of Highly Effective People*

This is a powerful tool for setting intentions that will support your greater self-awareness, expansion in consciousness and progress through the healing process. Start by making a brief list of the qualities you wish to cultivate in your life. Then write five or more statements describing what you want: What do you want now? What do really want? What do you really, really want?

I have used my own Life Mission Statement below as an example:

### EXAMPLE: *Clara's Life Mission Statement*

**Qualities:** Grace, Playfulness, Steadfastness

**What I really, really want NOW:**

To be Love

To live and share the principles of Spiritual Psychology

To seek and merit Divine Assistance and Guidance

To cultivate steadfastness and have clarity around my principles, life purpose and family life

To do what I say I want and/or intend to do

To be honest, decisive and authentic

To thrive personally, in my relationships and in my work

To experience fulfillment in my life, marriage and inside myself

To live fearlessly and enthusiastically

To sing, dance, play and laugh often

To be efficient and orderly in person and in work

To be proactive and bring things to completion

To be grateful

To be forgiving

To be flexible

To be creative

To be of Service

To SHINE!

## Devotion, Dedication, Discipline and Determination

The 4Ds – Devotion, Dedication, Discipline and Determination – are tools for our continued awakening. These are not actions we have to take, but qualities that simply are. We don't tell the flower to bloom; it just blooms. We don't put pressure on it. We don't plant a seed and tell it, "You have to bloom, flourish and be a beautiful flower." It just is. So, that would be the analogy we use with ourselves. By using these tools, we're not forcing ourselves into awakening. It just happens. We just feel it.

What is determination for you at this moment? What is dedication? How are you going to be disciplined? If you are addicted to pain, what does that mean in your life? Are you going to go back to dwelling in the negative thoughts, or are you going to choose something different? And how are you going to do that?

Are you devoted to your own awakening? To really awaken to who you are, you need determination. When you determine what it is you really, really want in your life, will you be devoted to the awakening? Do you have the discipline to meditate on gratitude and release the judgments every single night?

Are you willing to complete any cycles of action tonight and call it complete? Are you willing to see what the judgments are and do the forgiveness maintenance? Are you willing to forgive the judgments and then go to bed in peace and wake up and do three things that you're grateful for? Open yourself to that and see how the blessings and miracles show up in your life.

## Change Is One of
## Our Greatest Teachers

In order to live the life we want, we need to accept change as part of life. In this impermanent life, the two permanent things we are going to encounter for sure are death and change. In a sense, change is also a kind of death. We need to let go of the old to be able to receive the magic and blessings, that life has to offer.

Remember my Paris story about how my husband was so focused on his exhaustion that he was unable to recall what he'd enjoyed about our trip. He needed to let go of the pattern of focusing on the negative to be able to consciously allow himself to be happy and enjoy the happy moments. That was a change. A part of him needed to die to let the one who was happy emerge. I needed to awaken to the possibility that even though happiness and joy are sweeter when shared, my happiness didn't depend on his mood. We all have our own timing to awaken to who we really are.

To live an awakened life, we must be willing to make changes, and we must be willing to embrace death as a friend, an ally. Embracing unconditional self-forgiveness is accepting change and death. In a sense, it is embracing the idea that we consciously let the resentment go, die, dissolve, transform. It is like the caterpillar that transforms into a butterfly. Something changes, and in the process, we encounter beauty.

*"There are only two ways to live your life.*
*One is as though nothing is a miracle.*
*The other is as though everything is a miracle."*
—Albert Einstein

## One Last Story: Magic and Miracles

As I'm in the final process of finishing this book, I'm fully convinced that magic and miracles exist if we are open to them. I never had an engagement ring, but I considered my engagement ring to be a beautiful and very expensive watch my husband gave to me prior to our marriage.

Almost eight years ago, on a warm winter California night, my husband and I went out to the Jacuzzi in our housing complex, and that was the last time I saw the watch. I was deeply upset with myself. I was always super careful with all of my things. I wrote a note that I posted everywhere in our complex telling the story – my story – about how the watch meant so much more to me than its monetary worth.

I posted my note next to the pool and the Jacuzzi and diligently checked every day to see if someone had written a note in return or had left the watch for me to find. Sometimes the note was ripped apart or taken down completely. I didn't care. Methodically, I'd write the same story again and post it in the same places. A few of the people in my complex asked me why anyone would care what that watch meant to me! Sadly, the watch was not returned. After several years, we sold our house and since then have moved three times.

Last week when I was in the process of finishing this book, something happened. It was my son's birthday, and as I did every October

14th, I gave thanks to God for the life of my beautiful son. I asked God for something that was good. These last years, I have received beautiful messages, visions or experiences on October 14th.

On October 15th, my husband came home and did a magic trick, something he loves to do. He turned my white watch into the watch I'd lost so long ago. "What happened?" I asked without understanding what was going on. He said that a man who still lives near our old house had been trying to reach me without luck. He'd called my old number, gone to the old house and sent emails to a now defunct email address. So he finally contacted my husband.

He apologized and said that he was ashamed it had taken him so long to return my watch; he'd found it the night I lost it! When he saw my notes, he'd taken down my name and number, but when he got home, he put my contact information with the watch and stuck it somewhere for safekeeping. He'd intended to call me the next day, but then forgot about it. He had just found it in a kitchen drawer, still wrapped in the scrap of paper with my name and old contact information on it and decided to do everything he could to return it to me.

It was a funny feeling. That watch had been my companion for so many years, but hadn't been on my wrist for the most difficult years of my life. "This is closure," I thought. This is the sign. You never know when you will get what you want; things come to you in the right time. Don't judge the circumstances and never lose hope. Miracles and surprises are waiting for you around the corner. Ask, detach from the outcome, and be open and willing to receive.

## Forgiveness Test

At this point, you may want to revisit the forgiveness test in Chapter One to see how far you've progressed.

I also encourage you to giggle more and struggle less because, really, what is the purpose of life? To love and be happy... so let's use the forgiveness work to open the gates to inner liberation so we can be more loving toward ourselves and others, and experience the happiness that is already inside of us.

My daily prayer is: "God give me the strength to love myself as I love others, to forgive myself as I forgive others, to serve myself as I serve others and to see myself and others through your eyes."

I invite you now, in this moment, to write your own prayer.

May God Bless You!

✦ ✦ ✦

# EPILOGUE

*"We can complain because rose bushes have thorns,*
*or rejoice because thorn bushes have roses"*
—Abraham Lincoln

When I first thought about writing a book about forgiveness, I didn't know I was going to face such challenging circumstances in my own personal life. I didn't know, but my soul knew. As I developed my ideas, I realized that I wanted to share my own stories as well as the stories of my clients. Even as my faith was tested, I had the persistent desire to give a voice to the love that resides inside each of us.

As I write this epilogue, I'm witnessing on television Pope Francis' historic visit to the US. He is asking all of us how we can experience peace if we don't forgive and how we can expect to live just lives in the middle of injustices if we do not forgive. "Who am I to judge?" he asks. When we get to the point where we can ask ourselves, "Who am I to judge?" we don't need to forgive because we are already residing in that level of consciousness.

However, if we are not there yet, forgiveness clears us from the emotional debris that separates us from our own essence. By accepting our human essence and condition, we become aware of our divinity. Forgiveness is the tool that gives us hope and the ability to live fulfilling lives.

The crowds are enraptured by Pope Francis' passion, his message and his authenticity. His mission is love. The word "mission" ignites fire and excitement in my heart and brings tears to my eyes. My intention is, and has always been, to touch people's lives and hearts with the message of love.

This book is an open letter to the heart. By sharing stories that reflect a variety of life circumstances, and tools that lead to healing and awakening through forgiveness, it is my hope that your heart will open to love. We all have a song to sing, and the tune will be in harmony with your soul's mission when it comes from an open heart.

I'm writing and expressing now not from the crucifixion of suffering, resentment and shame, but from the other side of my own resurrection. We can experience resurrection when we are able to overcome suffering and pain. When I talk about crucifixion and resurrection, I'm not referring to them from a religious point of view. What I mean is that when we are in the middle of deep pain, sorrow or suffering, we are in a crucifixion condition and might be experiencing self-hatred, resentment, shame and guilt. When we overcome that condition, we experience our own rebirth or our own resurrection.

I realized that the only way I could share my experiences, my suffering and finally my resurrection, was to be utterly vulnerable. I asked myself if I should expose myself in such a manner. For what purpose? To inspire, I hope… To inspire you to let go of your feelings of shame, pain and self-judgment, to allow your own vulnerabilities to surface, for healing, for self-acceptance, for self-recognition. My intention is to empower you by encouraging you to embrace your perceived weaknesses, failures and mistakes, as well as your sorrow and pain. Ultimately, I hope to encourage you to be authentic... to dare to be you and know that you are never alone.

I hope by offering you the tools that have worked for me and my clients, you will also experience resurrection. By listening to the wisdom of your heart and rewriting the stories that have kept you a prisoner of pain and suffering, you will be able to experience an awakened heart and live a life of passion and compassion. Forgiveness is the key and the real meaning of the F-word.

In this convoluted world where people are persecuted for their beliefs, where so much poverty and hunger exists, we must forgive and embrace ourselves and each other with compassionate hearts in order to open up to the truth that God lives inside each one of us. Immersing yourself in the 3Fs process will shake your consciousness and lead you on a journey that takes you from fear to freedom, awakening your heart to unconditional love.

At the end of life, regardless of your beliefs, what really matters is how you lived, how much you served, how much you loved and how you experienced love. Forgiveness will crack open the heart and the light will shine.

This is the end of the book, but the journey has just begun.

*"People are often unreasonable, irrational, and self-centered. Forgive them anyway. If you are kind, people may accuse you of selfish, ulterior motives. Be kind anyway. If you are successful, you will win some unfaithful friends and some genuine enemies. Succeed anyway. If you are honest and sincere people may deceive*

*you. Be honest and sincere anyway. What you spend years creating, others could destroy overnight. Create anyway. If you find serenity and happiness, some may be jealous. Be happy anyway. The good you do today, will often be forgotten. Do good anyway. Give the best you have, and it will never be enough. Give your best anyway. In the final analysis, it is between you and God. It was never between you and them anyway."*

—Mother Teresa

✦ ✦ ✦

# ABOUT THE AUTHOR

Clara holds a Master of Arts degree in Spiritual Psychology from the University of Santa Monica, as well as Degrees in Business, Sociology, and International Business (the latter from the University of California Irvine). She is an International Certified Life Coach and has obtained a certification as a Soul Centered Professional  Coach from the University of Santa Monica. She is also trained as a Karuna and Usui Reiki Master, and is the founder of "The Kindness Movement," an online forum designed to inspire people around the world through kindness.

Formerly a Certified Public Accountant and a college professor, Clara now maintains a private practice in Newport Beach, California as a Transformational Consultant and Certified Professional Life Coach. She has developed her own unique and innovative style to help clients learn the power of forgiveness, personal responsibility and self-acceptance. She combines her years of experience in business with a positive and transformational approach to coaching and holistic counseling that integrates spiritual psychology, alternative healing therapies and powerful coaching tools.

Counseling inmates on a volunteer basis for the Freedom to Choose experiential prison program has been some of the most profound work of Clara's career. The Freedom to Choose program received a Hero Award in 2012, a national award presented by Agape, that recognizes excellence in prison reform programs.

Bilingual in English and Spanish, Clara grew up in Cordoba, Argentina. She hosts an interactive radio and Internet show there called "How to Live a Better Life," and has thousands of listeners in Latin America and the U.S. She also conducts workshops on forgiveness and personal growth in the United States, Argentina and Mexico.

Clara lives in California with her husband Sebastian. She enjoys spending time with her family, reading, and traveling the world. Her life purpose is to be of service, inspiring others to raise their consciousness as she continues the work of raising her own.

For more information on her workshops and her work, please visit

www.claranaum.com
claranaum@gmail.com

# SELECTED BIBLIOGRAPHY

Assagioli, Roberto, *Psychosynthesis A Manual of Principles and Techniques*. New York: Viking Press, 1971.

Borysenko, Joan. *Guilt is the Teacher, Love is the Lesson*. New York: Warner Book, 1988.

Borysenko Joan. *Mind the Body, Mending the Mind*. Massachusetts: Addison-Wesley, 1987.

Bradshaw, John. *Family Secrets, The Path to Self-Acceptance and Reunion*. New York: Bantam Books, 1995.

Covey, Stephen R. *The 7 Habits of Highly Effective People*. New York: Free Press, 1989, 2004.

Enright, Robert D. *Forgiveness is a Choice*. Washington: APA Life Tools, 2001.

Enright, Robert. *The Forgiving Life*. Washington: APA Life Tools, 2012.

Gwain Shakti, *Creative Visualization*. Berkeley CA. Whatever Pub, 1978.

Hay, Louise L. *You Can Heal Your Life*. Santa Monica, CA: Hay House, 1982.

Holden, Robert. *Success Intelligence*. Carlsbad CA. Hay House, 2005.

Hulnick H. Ronald and Hulnick Mary R. *Loyalty to your Soul, The Heart of Spiritual Psychology*. Hay House, 2011.

Levine, Peter A. *Trauma Through a Child's Eyes*. Berkeley, CA: 2007.

Lipton, Bruce H. *The Biology of Belief.* Carlsbad CA, Hay House, 2005.

Murphy, Joseph. *The Power of Your Subconscious Mind*. Radford, VA, 2007.

Myss, Caroline. *Anatomy of the Spirit*. New York: Random House, 1996.

Pransky, George S. *The Relationship Handbook*. La Conner, WA: Pransky and Associates, P.S.

Roger John with Kaye, Paul. *Living the Spiritual Principles of Health and Well-Being*. Los Angeles, CA. Mandeville Press, 2010.

Siegel Bernie S. *Love, Medicine and Miracles*. New York: Harper Collins, 1991.

Weil, Andrew. *Health and Healing: Understanding Conventional and Alternative Medicine*. Boston: Houghton Mifflin, 1983.

# NOTES

# NOTES

# NOTES

# NOTES

# NOTES

# NOTES

58992076R00136

Made in the USA
Lexington, KY
22 December 2016